LIFE
Scripts

Remedies From
One Healer to Another

LIFE

Scripts

Remedies From
One Healer to Another

Learn to Heal Yourself,
Take Charge of Your Happiness,
Change Negatives to Positives and
Create a Better Life

DONNA LEVI

Please Remember to Leave an Amazon Review :)

Hello New Friend!
I'm so excited to go on this Life Scripts journey together!
If this book helps you, even in the smallest way,
to look at life differently, find a little happiness,
or live a more fulfilled life,
then I'd love to hear about it!

It only takes a few seconds...

Simply scan the below
QR code to leave an
Amazon rating and/or review:

or go to this link:
amzn.to/3BRQclc

Thank you so much!

For a free sampling of my next book,
giveaways, collaborations,
reviews or latest news,
email me!

DonnaLeviBooks@gmail.com

Also by Donna Levi

The
HEALERS TRILOGY:

The Healers
(The Healers Trilogy, Book 1)
Link: https://amzn.to/3amRbib

Waters of Life
(The Healers Trilogy, Book 2)
Link: https://amzn.to/3yTyCvu

Crystal Caverns
(The Healers Trilogy, Book 3)
Link: https://amzn.to/3yS3fkK

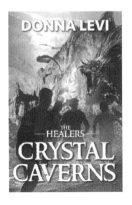

Life Scripts
Copyright © 2022 Donna Levi

Book Design Layout: Platinum Publicity

Life Scripts
Donna Levi

Library of Congress Control Number: 2021920390
ISBN: 978-0-9885526-5-4

LIFE
Scripts

Dedicated to
my Goldendoodle, Buddy,
who has been my comfort and source of
unconditional love for the past ten years.
He has brought healing energy to
everyone he has ever met.

"We are all works in progress with
specific gifts that become apparent
as soon as we allow them
entrance into our lives.

So be brave.
You are not alone.
You are a healer."

- Donna Levi

CONTENTS

CHAPTER 4: HEALING

CHAPTER 5: THE ART OF GIVING AND RECEIVING

CHAPTER 6: HOW TO LOVE

CHAPTER 7: CHANGING NEGATIVES TO POSITIVES

CHAPTER 8: FACING CHALLENGES

CHAPTER 9: ACCEPTING THE GUIDANCE AROUND YOU

CHAPTER 10: HOW TO CREATE A BETTER LIFE

CHAPTER 11: SURVIVING AND LOVING THE HOLIDAYS

My
Life
Script

Finding My Purpose: A Personal Story of Transformation

My Life *Script*

How I Found My Purpose:
A Personal Story of Transformation

———— • • • ————

Do you know who you are?

My guess is that you are a healer.

Healers come in all shapes and sizes, ages and genders, occupations, religions, and nationalities. The potential is within us all. Just because you haven't discovered your healing abilities, or even considered that you have such talents, does not mean that you are without them. You simply need to recognize that spark of healing energy inside. Once you do, you will be more able to easily fan into the brilliant light that is you.

This book may open your eyes to your True purpose.

Through these "scripts" ("prescriptions"), which spotlight the events and emotions that we grapple with daily, I hope that you will see yourself more clearly. Once armed with that information, you can choose to hold steady with what is working in your life and let go of the stuff that is not.

Sometimes, a thoughtful moment and an open heart is all it takes to move us toward healing ourselves - and others.

I became aware of my gifts, my potential, and my purpose through a lengthy process. I didn't mind. That's how we grow. And only when I look back over the past several years do I realize what an amazing transformation I experienced.

After years in the business world, I was trying my hand at being a stay-at-home mom. I quickly realized that, even though I deeply loved my children, I had chosen the hardest job on the planet! With a four-year-old on one hip, a two-year-old on the other, an ailing mother with dementia, an elderly father living on his own, and a husband working hard to pay the bills,

I lost myself completely.
I no longer had an identity.

Who was I?

Did I have a purpose outside of "caregiver"?

I felt drained, an empty shell of a human being.

My mother died the following year. The emptiness that already gripped me quickly became full-blown depression. And my despair grew more difficult to ignore and to function around with each passing day. I felt terribly disappointed, even angry that she had left me. Though my children needed my care, I could not fight the whirlpool of loneliness pulling me down.

I was drowning.

My emotions began to manifest themselves physically. Every month, like clockwork, I fell ill with something like strep throat. Knowing what I know now, I realize my illnesses were from not speaking my truth, not expressing my feelings.

In 2009, I celebrated my thirty-ninth birthday. Around that time, my life got especially interesting. My sister planned a trip and asked if I would join her. She knew I needed a break from the internal maelstrom that had rendered me nearly unrecognizable, at least to myself. She thought if she could encourage me to take some time away, even for a couple of days, I might start viewing life differently.

I, of course, was reluctant to even entertain the thought of leaving with two small children at home. I had responsibilities. And how would my husband feel about the added duties? But after mulling over her offer for a time, I made a command decision. I was going! I was going to go on a trip with my sister! Everyone was just going to have to make do without me for a few days. Besides, an emotionally healthier mom and wife is always a better one.

Turns out, my sister had booked us at an award-winning wellness retreat called Canyon Ranch in Tucson, Arizona.

And in that calm, nurturing environment, I did some soul-searching.

On paper, my life seemed to be nearly perfect. In reality, it was not.

So . . . what was missing?

What was the missing piece?

I didn't know what the piece looked like, so finding it had eluded me. While at the resort, I decided to schedule a service called "healing touch." For many years, I had been interested in metaphysical and spiritual development, but "energy medicine" was a new concept to me. This process of healing another individual of emotional and physical blockages using only the healing energy inherent in each of our bodies and minds was positively fascinating.

After arriving back home, my "real" life once again took over, and I ignored everything I had learned on my trip, putting my personal evolution on hold. Subsequently, I once again became very ill. My doctor prescribed stronger and stronger antibiotics, but I continued to get worse.

I got to the point where I was afraid to go to sleep for fear that I would not wake.

Desperation and survival instincts kicked in.

I laid in bed thinking,

"There must be a way for me to heal myself because the medicine isn't working."

At that moment, something miraculous happened. The instant I had that thought, the idea, characters, and practically the outline for what became my first book flooded my mind in rapid succession. It would be a story about a small band of children from various parts of the globe, each with their own healing abilities, teaching others to heal their own lives.

So crisp and clear was my vision for the book that the following morning I was compelled to sort it out with pen and paper. I finally found what I had been searching for: a greater purpose in life, an identity, a creative outlet with which I could express my true self while spreading a message of hope and love to humanity.

In a universe of unlimited possibility and abundance, I had attracted what I was ready to receive.

My illness and depression evaporated. Writing about these young people who were born to heal the world was my healing.

We are all works in progress with specific gifts that become apparent as soon as we allow them entrance into our lives. So be brave. You are not alone. You are a healer. And your healing presence has the power to awaken the grand potential in others. Because ultimately, we are all the same: expressions of pure love and light.

I've learned much since that fated thirty-ninth birthday. For instance, I now understand that we all possess the strength to better our lives and that attitude is everything. I realize how vital it is to listen to what life is telling me and to lead with my heart. I recognize more readily when it's time to let go, to ask for what I need, and to be open to accepting the Universe's answer to each request. And I've learned that life is a perfectly orchestrated symphony of good and bad, and that every moment presents a fresh opportunity to listen and learn. Now I want to share that knowledge while encouraging and inspiring you to be the extraordinary person you were born to be.

The essays gathered in this book were all inspired by my light-bulb moment. Think of them as over-the-counter prescriptions (scripts) for happiness, each focused exclusively on your wellness, your brilliance, and helping you discover every opportunity to enhance your life and create a better world. .

Just some loving, tenured advice
- from one healer to another.

Your
Life
Script

How to Use this Book for
Your Personal
Transformation Journey

Your Life *Script*

How to Use This Book For
Your Personal Transformation Journey

— • • —

This collection of articles is here to serve as "life prescriptions" over-the-counter advice on how you can regain and/or develop the skills needed to experience your very best life.

Each Life Script offers guidance that's easy to digest, retain, and implement. And, as added support, you will find a "Take Action" Worksheet after every Life Script, providing you with tangible tools to put the advice into motion in your life.

These actionable worksheets present you with easy to start first steps towards your healing journey. Be honest with yourself in these exercises. No one is judging you.

There is no right or wrong way
to go about healing with Life Scripts.

Your worksheets can also act as your own personal journal for you to study, revise and reread as you travel along your healing path.

Each Life Script and its worksheet is specifically designed to stand alone, so you can decide if you are going to work through this book in order, or start by focusing on the Life Script topic that most speaks to what you're going through right this moment.

Each chapter covers a specific theme, making it simple to find a healing prescription for whatever problem you may be struggling with on any given day.

For example, if you want more joy, you can jump to **Chapter 2: "Taking Charge of Your Happiness."** Here you'll find **Script 8: "Do You Really Know What Joy Is?"** where I help you determine what joy is, what it is not, and how to find it. Then the **Take Action Worksheet** will guide you through actually putting into action what you just learned.

If negative emotions are impacting your life, you can flip to the Scripts in **Chapter 7: "Changing Negatives to Positives."** There you'll find Life Scripts #32 - #37 to combat feeling unloved, imprisoned by circumstance, or not being good enough, and you'll learn how to mend those wounds.

"Harnessing the Law of Attraction" in **Chapter 3** discusses not only manifesting what you want but how to STOP manifesting what you don't (Script #15). And then the worksheet will help you take action steps to do it!

The Life Scripts in **"Surviving and Loving the Holidays"** in **Chapter 11** point out ways to minimize the performance anxiety of gift-giving and family expectations and to embrace each occasion with a happy heart.

Chapter 8's "Facing Challenges" covers Scripts on how to cope with frustration (Script #38), how to deflect those who push your buttons (Script #39), and the role fear can play in your life-if you let it (Script #40).

I've been there. And, like you, I'm a work-in-progress. But I learned that I already possessed the ability to heal much of what impeded my personal growth by taking the "prescriptions" outlined in this book. And now, fellow healer, I want to pass the power to you. I want you, too, to learn that you have the ability to heal, and I hope this book starts you along your healing journey.

Remember, you may not know this yet, but you are a healer. You have the ability to tend to the wounds of yourself and other people. Maybe you don't know how to set a broken bone, but you can "doctor" the emotional and spiritual damage inflicted on those around you. However, you won't be able to exercise that gift of yours until you first heal yourself.

WARNING: Your happiness may be habit-forming.

Xoxo,
Donna Levi

"Never fear being different from
those around you.

Their journey is theirs,
just as yours is yours.

Everyone has a story,
and no two are the same."

- Donna Levi

CHAPTER 1

Embracing
Who You Are

Life
Script

#1

How is Your
Life *Really* Going?

How is Your Life *Really* Going

So, how is your life going?

Do you feel like you've been doing everything right?

Probably not. You help those who are less fortunate, are kind to animals, and are definitely all about world peace. Yet you struggle through life and watch as others, who seemingly do not have your pure, loving heart, enjoy happy, prosperous lives, and you think,

"Why not me?"

> Well, I happen to strongly believe that when good people suffer greatly, it means they have a great destiny and mission to fulfill in this lifetime.

It isn't enough to just talk the talk, we have to walk the walk —in other people's shoes—if we want to make a huge difference in this world.

Let's examine three positive reasons why we may be going through discomfort, uncertainty, and pain in our lives:

1. NECESSARY PREPARATION

Has it ever occurred to you that because of who you are and who you are supposed to be, that you were hand-picked and are somehow being groomed for a position of grand significance? Have you thought that experiencing certain feelings at a deep level, all the way to the core of your soul, is a prerequisite for that particular "job" on this planet?

*It could be that a life-changing event
you don't see and can't imagine
is being lined up for you in the very near future,*

someone or something that will require your full attention. If you've lived through that particular challenge, you will absolutely feel more up to the task than if you have no understanding of what is required in that certain situation.

Recognize that most charitable organizations in the world were established because of someone's deep and fearless determination to put all of their focus and energy into an issue that profoundly affected their lives. One such person is the founder of MADD (Mothers Against Drunk Driving), Candy Lightner. She lost a daughter to a drunk driver, which ignited her passion to change the world in a positive way.

*The Universe trusted her to make something
new and good out of her pain.*

*That pain brought her into the
fullness of her destiny.*

Maybe you have always had a comfortable life, never worried too much about money, but now, your wealth is in question. Consider that we are in a new age when it is imperative to know and feel and understand what it's like for people who can't pay their bills. It could be that your new financial concerns are a test of your compassion for your fellow human being. Possibly, feeling the pain of someone who has been scraping by their whole life is what is required to prepare you for the responsibility of great prosperity. And with that prosperity, you might be able to bring momentous change to the fairness of our entire monetary system or turn the public's attention to how we treat one another, whether a person has money or not.

Pain in every form has a purpose. When you experience great pain, you need to get ready for a new level of understanding offering fresh opportunities. Trust, have patience, and learn from the lesson shown to you.

2. APPRECIATION

At some point, all of us have taken for granted our blessings. Count a few of them. Do you have a job, home, healthy children, money, a partner? If you do, do you regularly recognize those gifts as being the big deal that they are? We probably don't do that as much as we should.

If everything is always rosy, how can we ever truly appreciate all of that good fortune?

So, when some part of our life that we have been taking for granted is suddenly lost, our health, money, marriage, and so on, heed that major lesson.

Through hardship we learn to appreciate every little thing in life, don't we?

Every inch of our day-to-day existence becomes important. We become mindful and grateful,

and sometimes the lesson is so big for us that we never take our blessings for granted again.

Maybe the experience of a health scare or potential breakup or even the threat of divorce has lifted anger and resentment toward another person from you because you now appreciate the importance of having them in your life.

Could this be another way that the Universe, God, a Higher Power is entrusting you with a grand mission? And now you are able to handle the responsibility of what will be given to you because you have learned how precious the gifts of life are, unlike before you felt the discomfort?

Keep an open mind. I believe that there are no accidents. You are being elevated in consciousness whenever you gain awareness and realize something new about your life.

3. REMOVING A CRUTCH

The material world in which we exist is full of crutches.

What I mean is that there are things on which we rely that do not come from within but from the external world around us. Maybe you are using something or someone in your life as a type of "security blanket." To make any profound change in your life, you have to detach from this person or thing before you can start depending on your innate abilities and have faith in the unseen.

Most of us have some kind of crutch or security blanket that allows us to avoid living up to our full potential. .

Our lives may require a bit of letting go and some uncomfortable feelings of loss to bring about our highest good.

Perhaps you have been too focused on accumulating all your "stuff," or maybe you've been too dependent on another person for your needs. This type of behavior leads to complacency, staying in the same place in your life from year to year and not moving forward to where you are destined to go. Sometimes a little suffering goes a long way in propelling a person to their greatness.

Is it possible that one or all of the above three reasons resonates with you in your current circumstances?

Have you already lived to tell about a situation that happened in your life and can help a person who is going through something similar right now?

Either way, the unpleasant side of life gives us a lot to feel and think about, but I guarantee, we become stronger, wiser, and better human beings because of it.

LET'S TAKE ACTION! WORKSHEET:

Reframing Hardships

Let's practice reframing our hardships into positives!

1 PREPARATION:

Can you think of a time in your past when a hardship actually turned out to be necessary preparation for something that happened later in life? What was it?

_____

_____

_____

Think of a current challenge you are facing, but let's reframe it into a positive - What could this challenge be preparing you for in the future? Don't be afraid to get creative or think big!

_____

_____

_____

Keep it up: Try practicing this for every hardship in your life! It may be difficult at first, but every challenge can be seen in a positive light!

2. APPRECIATION:

What are 5 gifts in your life that you sometimes forget to appreciate?

Can you think of a time when you almost lost, or did lose, something in your life, and then afterwards learned to appreciate that thing even more? What was it and how did it feel? Did you end up continuing to appreciate that thing, or did you lose appreciation for it again over time? Write about it below:

Keep it up: Every morning, write a list of 3 things you appreciate, from the littlest things to the biggest - and everything in between!

3. CRUTCH

Can you think of something in your life that letting go of (even though it would be uncomfortable) could bring about something better? What's stopping you?

You did it! Congrats! 👏

Life
Script
#2

Why Being Dedicated to
Your Personal *Growth*
is So Important

Why Being Dedicated to Your Personal *Growth* is So Important

— • • • —

Carrying around emotional baggage is a heavy burden to bear, and letting go of that extra stuff is an integral part of our journey on this planet. Unfortunately, at one point or another, we all have to face the fact that our lives aren't going to get better until we deal with our issues.

Try an "Emotional Clean-Up"

An emotional "clean up" of one's life can be difficult at best, but the results of making a concerted effort to do so will completely change you and send you where you're supposed to be, which is toward living an amazing, fulfilling, joyful life.

What needs healing on the outside has to be addressed at the roots.

Of course, that's easier said than done. Inner healing requires a willingness and commitment to finding out why your life is the way it is, what you need to do to change it for the better, and then making those changes. (We'll be working on all that good stuff here in this book!)

The bottom line is, most people resist. They don't want to admit that they're leading a less-than-fulfilling life, and they surely don't want to hear that the responsibility for that, as well as the means to alter it, lies directly within them. It's easier to place blame outside of ourselves, especially if someone has hurt us deeply. But the fact remains that if you are giving someone else the power to control your happiness, then that is on you—not them. And giving away your power does more than hurt you; it prevents you from being able to help anyone else.

The following three points are important to recognize and consider in order to put an end to a possibly lifelong cycle of discontentment and to embrace the necessity for personal growth.

1. AM I BEING HONEST WITH MYSELF

If something major is not working in your life, you have to admit that truth to yourself.

Trying to overlook a traumatic situation that happened to you in the past or a current situation that is making you terribly unhappy is never going to move you toward your goal of finding fulfillment.

Denial does not work, and you are not fooling anyone, particularly yourself.

You are not going to deal with your issues simply by ignoring them. The situation will haunt you, day in and day out, whether you consciously acknowledge it or not. It will tap you on the shoulder every chance it gets and say, "Pay attention to me!" It will demand your attention and focus until you deal with it.

Having those feelings pent up inside begging you to address them is preventing you from having the life you want, and in fact may be guaranteeing that you never live the amazing life you are supposed to be living. Instead, you will continue to project and carry dysfunction into all of your relationships and then wonder why they are a mess, whether relationships with your partner, kids, parents, friends, or anyone else.

There are countless self-help books (like this one!), spiritual materials, and counselors ready to help you through this process of healing. But those resources can't help if you don't take advantage of them and the opportunity they provide to heal.

2. AM I FOCUSED ON THE WRONG THINGS?

What you are in alignment with is what you are going to get. How many of us are convinced that we are centered when we clearly are not? It doesn't matter how well you think you can fake it by smiling and acting jovial. Your vibration can still be quite low and feel crappy to everyone around you.

Not only that, no matter how happy you pretend to be, the Universe is not easily fooled.

We all just want to jump straight to the future where we will be fulfilled and all of our dreams will manifest, but that cannot happen until we align ourselves with those goals.

If you are focused on that which gives you a feeling of well-being, wholeness, and contentment, then you are in alignment and your needs can be met by the Universe. This can be done by trusting and allowing the Divine Order of all things.

However, if you are living in a constant state of worry, want, and resistance, then you are out of alignment with the flow of creation, and your needs will forever remain beyond your reach.

The Universe will always provide for what resonates within us. We cannot experience what does not, and this is how desires become blocked from manifesting.

The Universe is a mirror.

It does one thing; it responds to our focus, which in turn dictates our vibration, our resonance.

Change your focus, and the Universe will change its response.

3. YOUR PERSONAL GROWTH REACHES FAR BEYOND YOU

I frequently hear people say, "I know I want to help the world in some way, but I don't really know what to do. I should be in Africa helping people or something."

First of all, if that were true, you'd be in Africa.

You are where you are supposed to be at this moment.

Maybe someday you will be in Africa or somewhere else helping others, but right now, there is something extremely important that you must hear:

Your growth is your service.

What does that mean? It means that every single time you choose to love, heal, shift, evolve, and allow your authenticity to lead the way, you are supporting the whole of the planet in more profound ways than you could ever imagine.

When you decide to commit to healing the core of your being, to growing and transmuting into the light that your soul wants you to be, then you shift not only the energy in your own life (dramatically for the better),

but you also raise the vibrational frequency of the entire planet.

Therefore, when you work on yourself, you'll enjoy a better life while also serving everyone and everything around you in the process.

Daily, we all need to remind ourselves that we attract what we do because of who we are being.

Can we attract opportunities if our focus is on the absence of opportunities in our life?

No.

Can we attract love with a closed heart?

No.

If our habitual thoughts are negative, will we create a positive outcome?

No.

Who are you being, and who do you truly want to be?

Be honest. Every person on the planet needs to work on themselves for myriad reasons. There are no exceptions. Anyone who insists that they are immune to this reality is going to stay stagnant and stuck in a life that inspires struggle and despair.

LET'S TAKE ACTION! WORKSHEET:

Let's be honest!

Are you being honest with yourself? Explain why or why not:
(Refer back to #1 in this script.)

_____

_____

_____

Are you focused on the wrong things? Explain why or why not:
(Refer back to #2 in this script.)

_____

_____

_____

Do you recognize that your personal growth reaches far beyond you?
Explain why or why not: (Refer back to #3 in this script.)

_____

_____

_____

What feelings, reflections or thoughts did this chapter bring up for you?
Write it below:

_____

_____

_____

Life
Script
Rx #3

What *Kind* of Person
Are You?

What *Kind* of Person Are You?

Only you can determine the type of person you are and what you stand for. No one else can decide this for you. It has nothing to do with your status, job, influence, or wealth. Whichever "type" resonates with you is YOUR truth.

But will that be the case in five months? Five years? Maybe. Maybe not.

To answer that, ask yourself this question:

On what are you choosing to shine your light?

Because whatever burns brightest within us will light the space around us,

whether it is love, peace, pain, fear, or sadness.

It emanates and illuminates our hearts and environment like a gigantic floodlight.

So, in determining what type of person you are, think about what you are choosing to focus on at this time in your life and during this particular point in history. What are you bringing to the planet, your neighborhood, your family?

Be honest! Do NOT judge your answer. This is just where you are choosing to be right now.

1. THOSE WHO FEEL
MORE IMPORTANT THAN OTHERS

This describes an ego-centered individual who believes that because of their position, bank account, ethnicity, etc. that they are better than someone else, that they are, therefore, entitled to receive more, and that some people are replaceable or disposable. They feel that certain people's lives matter more than others.

> *This type of person favors his or her wants at the expense of the higher good of all.*

It's an "us against them" fear-based mentality. This individual is all about themselves and those like them. They are actively against those who are not similar to them.

It wouldn't hurt for them to "wear another person's shoes" once in a while.

2. THOSE WHO FEEL
LESS IMPORTANT THAN OTHERS

This person feels a lack of self-love and self-worth,

> *always putting others above themselves, rarely thinking that they are valuable or worthy enough to receive.*

They see others as better than they are in any number of ways: prettier, wealthier, smarter, happier, skinnier, and so on. This type of individual is for others but against themselves, because they believe they are not good enough.

They could benefit a great deal from looking within and realizing the power and perfection they truly possess.

3. THOSE WHO FEEL EQUAL IN IMPORTANCE TO THOSE AROUND THEM

This type of person believes that we are all ONE. They perceive that the light on the planet is increasing, even if the news suggests otherwise. They see between the lines. They are aware of the love that is spreading. They acknowledge the helpers—strangers assisting and showing love and kindness to strangers.

They believe we are all connected.

The color of our skin, our gender, our sexual orientation, our beliefs, our economic status—none of it matters because we are all the same at our core.

YEP, YOU FALL INTO ONE OF THOSE CATEGORIES.

Now, your position may change over time. A particular event can have us reestablishing how we view ourselves. Other times, that assessment can change merely because we stop and consider our behavior and beliefs. But more and more people are resonating with the third option listed.

As humanity's strength and fragility are brought to our attention through TV, radio, and social media as we witness individuals on earth sacrificing their lives, and as we, ourselves, lose loved ones, the suffering is the same. Our nationalities are irrelevant. An influx of compassion and deeper understanding is the result.

At this time, horrific events are taking place across the planet. But notice how we as human beings are using these events to feel more deeply and increase our compassion for one another. No one EVER dies in vain.

As individuals, and as a collective, we are evolving in our perceptions and elevating into higher consciousness. Our choices—how we respond to and utilize challenging events for the greater good of all living things—is what propels humanity to a higher level of understanding, which is only LOVE.

So many are beginning to feel love for one another on a soul level, not just on a human level. The power of love is growing, and we are growing as individual beings of light. We are expanding our awareness to include every person in unity and harmony, no longer wanting to live in fear and separation. We search for the light in every situation no matter how terrible it seems, always finding the good and the love that spreads in the wake of any disaster.

Greater numbers of people throughout the world are noticing the shift in a profound, powerful, and positive way. They know that one day our choices will be such that no one will consider harming another bright soul, not even for a moment, because we will all choose to make full use of our capacity for conscious and compassionate behavior.

As human beings, we were given the gifts of intelligence, conscience, and free will. Therefore, we have a responsibility to ALL life.

We are expected to act not blindly or selfishly, but with a higher consciousness built upon a secure moral and spiritual foundation.

I used to be the second type, but now I'm the third. I value myself now as much as I value other dear souls. How can you possibly be a beacon of love and light for others without seeing it inside of YOU? In fact, shining your love-light is indeed the most important job and biggest purpose you can ever fulfill in this life.

LET'S TAKE ACTION! WORKSHEET:

What is motivating you?

① Which category do you think you may fit into at this stage of your life: #1, #2 or #3? Circle one (there's no wrong answer!)

② For a few days, keep the below journal of all your actions and the motivation behind them. At the end of three days, sit down with your journal and reflect upon its revelations. You may discover a new awareness of how consciously or unconsciously you are living your life and what actions and thoughts may no longer resonate with who you are — or who you want to be.

Day 1:

Action:

1.

2.

3.

Motivation behind the action:

1.

2.

3.

Day 2:

Action:

1.

2.

3.

Motivation behind the action:

1.

2.

3.

Day 3:

Action:

1.

2.

3.

Motivation behind the action:

1.

2.

3.

3 End of Day 3 Reflections:

Go back through your actions and motivations over the last 3 days. Did you have any revelations? Did you discover a new awareness of how consciously or unconsciously you are living your life and what actions and thoughts may no longer resonate with who you are right now, or who you want to be? Did the answer to which category you belong in change?

Reflect below:

_____

_____

_____

_____

_____

_____

_____

_____

_____

_____

_____

_____

_____

_____

_____

_____

_____

_____

Great Work!

Life
Script
#4

How *Mature* Are You?

How *Mature* Are You?

———— • • • ————

Do you think there is a certain age at which maturity sets in?

Could it be twenty?

Forty?

Seventy?

In my personal experiences, I've observed that age has little or nothing to do with maturity.

I have met young people who are mature well beyond their years, and older folks who act childish, only thinking about themselves. But what are the character traits that show maturity? And do "mature" people exhibit those behaviors all of the time?

I'm not sure that any of us do.

No matter our age, we're always growing and learning as human beings,

and I'm pretty sure that everyone has been guilty of childish behavior at least once or twice. That being said, by considering these twenty-five attributes of maturity, perhaps we can become more aware of the interludes in which our whiny, adolescent selves rear their immature little heads.

But what are the characteristics of Maturity?

25 ATTRIBUTES OF MATURITY:

1) Realizing how much you don't know

2) Listening more and talking less

3) Considering others, as opposed to being self-absorbed, self-centered, and, well, inconsiderate

4) Not taking everything personally, getting easily offended, or feeling the need to defend, prove, or make excuses for yourself

5) Being grateful and gracious, not complaining

6) Taking responsibility for your own health and happiness, not relying on others to "fix" you, or placing blame for your circumstances

7) Having forgiveness and compassion for yourself and others

8) Being calm, peaceful, and patient, not desperate, frantic, or irrational

9) Showing flexibility and openness, as opposed to being resistant, controlling, or unreasonable

10) Helping yourself, not expecting others to do things for you out of a sense of entitlement

11) Doing good deeds even when there is nothing in it for you other than knowing you helped; being selfless

12) Respecting another's point of view, beliefs, and way of life without judgment, not insisting you are right, belittling the other person, or using profanity or violence to get your point across

13) Sharing your good fortune with others

14) Being able to turn the other cheek without wishing harm on another

15) Thinking before acting and having good manners, not going off half-cocked, lashing out, or being rude

16) Encouraging and being supportive of others

17) Finding joy in someone else's success, not envy or criticism

18) Knowing there is always room to grow and improve and reaching out for help

19) Having humility and laughing at yourself

20) Recognizing that which does not work in your life and making an effort to do those things differently

21) Passing up instant gratification in favor of long-term benefits

22) Accepting, liking, and loving yourself, not needing someone else to "complete" you

23) Standing up for fairness and justice for yourself and others and choosing to do the right thing, no matter how difficult

24) Making sacrifices for the good of others without resentment

25) Not clinging to materialistic items or bragging

I think the most important practice is to regularly check in with our developed self and recognize the negative side of our behavior, then make a positive move toward changing it.

SO LET'S PRACTICE CHECKING IN WITH OURSELVES RIGHT NOW. . .

Can you recognize the positive & negative sides of your behavior in the check list on the next page?

LET'S TAKE ACTION! WORKSHEET:

Attributes of Maturity
- Check List Challenge -

Below is a list from the Twenty-Five Attributes of Maturity. Check the box next to each one to see where you fit on the maturity scale:

✓ Check the ♡ box for "Yes!"

✓ Check the ⚠ box If you're working on it

Remember this check list is not an exercise to criticize or get angry with ourselves. It's just to check in with ourselves and recognize our behaviors. Then we can make a positive move toward changing them for the better.

	Yes!	I'm working on it!
I realize how much I don't know.	♡	⚠
I listen more and talk less.	♡	⚠
I consider others.	♡	⚠
I'm not self-absorbed.	♡	⚠
I'm not self-centered.	♡	⚠
I'm not inconsiderate.	♡	⚠
I don't take everything personally.	♡	⚠
I don't get easily offended.	♡	⚠
I don't feel the need to defend everything.	♡	⚠
I don't feel the need to prove anything.	♡	⚠
I don't feel the need to make excuses for myself.	♡	⚠

47

	Yes!	I'm working on it!
I'm grateful.	♡	⚠
I'm gracious.	♡	⚠
I don't complain.	♡	⚠
I take responsibility for my own health and happiness, not relying on others to "fix" me.	♡	⚠
I don't place blame for my circumstances on others.	♡	⚠
I have forgiveness and compassion for others.	♡	⚠
I have forgiveness and compassion for myself.	♡	⚠
I am calm.	♡	⚠
I am peaceful.	♡	⚠
I am patient.	♡	⚠
I am not desperate.	♡	⚠
I am not frantic.	♡	⚠
I am not irrational.	♡	⚠
I am flexible.	♡	⚠
I am open.	♡	⚠
I am not resistant.	♡	⚠
I am not controlling.	♡	⚠
I am not unreasonable.	♡	⚠

Life Scripts

	Yes!	I'm working on it!
I help myself.	♡	⚠
I don't expect others to do things for me out of a sense of entitlement.	♡	⚠
I do good deeds even when there is nothing in it for me other than knowing I helped.	♡	⚠
I try to be selfless.	♡	⚠
I respect others' points of view, beliefs, and way of life without judgment.	♡	⚠
I don't insist I'm right.	♡	⚠
I don't belittle other people.	♡	⚠
I don't use profanity or violence to get my point across.	♡	⚠
I don't place blame for my circumstances on others.	♡	⚠
I share my good fortune with others.	♡	⚠
I am able to turn the other cheek without wishing harm on another.	♡	⚠
I think before acting.	♡	⚠
I have good manners.	♡	⚠
I don't lash out.	♡	⚠
I encourage and support others.	♡	⚠
I find joy in someone else's success.	♡	⚠
I don't envy or criticize someone else's success.	♡	⚠

	Yes!	I'm working on it!
I know there's always room to grow and improve.	♡	⚠
I reach out for help when I need it.	♡	⚠
I have humility.	♡	⚠
I can laugh at myself.	♡	⚠
I recognize that which does not work in my life.	♡	⚠
I make an effort to do those things differently.	♡	⚠
I pass up instant gratification in favor of long-term benefits.	♡	⚠
I accept myself.	♡	⚠
I like myself.	♡	⚠
I love myself.	♡	⚠
I don't need someone else to "complete" me.	♡	⚠
I stand up for fairness and justice for myself and others.	♡	⚠
I choose to do the right thing, no matter how difficult.	♡	⚠
I make sacrifices for the good of others.	♡	⚠
I am not materialistic.	♡	⚠
I don't brag.	♡	⚠

Wow you did it!!!!! 👏

How did it go?

How do you think your maturity level stacks up?

What are your positive takeaways?

Did you find some attributes you could improve?

Did you stumble upon some positive aspects you forgot to give yourself credit for?

Let's start appreciating our good qualities, while also making some positive changes!

Keep it up: Put a reminder in your calendar every month to refer back to this maturity list and see how your check marks change over time.

Life
Script
#5

How to Allow Others to Walk
Their Own Path

How to Allow Others to Walk Their Own Path

I believe that this beautiful planet of ours is a very large school and that each of us has signed up to take different subjects specifically designed for our chosen "degrees" throughout our lifetimes. Some courses can be easy and others extremely difficult.

What is highly important to note is that no matter how much we desire to make others' lives easier or feel the need to explain our choices, we have to understand that each and every individual, including ourselves and our children, has their own path to traverse.

We have to be who we truly are and let others do the same.

If we always shelter people, we end up doing their lessons for them so they never have to feel pain. Thus, they are doomed to repeat those lessons until they have been learned. And if we always edit our lives and shove our dreams under the table to please others, we are missing out on experiences we should be having. Sometimes, all we do is hinder the soul's progress, which certainly isn't anyone's intention.

So even though we're just trying to be helpful or "keep the peace,"

we must recognize that most of the time it's a good idea to simply take a step back

and let life happen as it should before deciding to step in. Look at the list below and consider what is motivating you.

1. WHETHER TO GIVE ASSISTANCE OR TOUGH LOVE

Human suffering is difficult to witness. It pulls at our heartstrings to know that another human being is hungry, cold, or in desperate need of basic comfort in any way. It is a beautiful thing to care for others, to be compassionate and give of yourself and your possessions, to alleviate the suffering of someone you may not even know.

This type of act, this service to humanity spreads love and healing throughout the world. This is definitely a positive and glorious display of the innate goodness of the human heart. However, you have to first believe that

You giving another human being assistance will create a positive shift in their lives and that they will pay that kindness forward with love and gratitude.

On the other hand, let's say that a friend or relative has gotten into some pretty serious trouble with the law for something they've done. Maybe they call you from jail asking for you to bail them out. Or perhaps someone you know has gambled away their paycheck and needs you to cover their expenses. Maybe your kid hasn't been doing his or her homework and needs you to make up excuses to the teacher on their behalf.

Even though you may want to fix the situation for these people,

THE REAL QUESTION IN EACH OF THESE SCENARIOS IS:

Would you be doing them a monumental disservice if you did?

Bailing people out and covering for them in order for them to avoid the consequences of their actions is not helping them at all. In fact, it's harmful because the situation will be brought back to them again and again until whatever lesson being taught has been learned.

You deny them the opportunity to use their experiences to change their lives for the better.

Yes, it is frustrating.

You want to jump in and rescue and protect, but people have to take responsibility for their choices.

Sitting with consequences, feeling them, is how we learn.

Challenges in life are necessary for transformation.

They test us, reshape us, and bring us closer to our authentic selves. This is not true suffering; this is self-inflicted misery.

2. KNOWING AND PROVING ARE NOT THE SAME

Do you know who and what you are, or do you live your life seeking the approval of others? If you feel yourself needing to prove something, that is a sure sign that you have given your power away.

Defending and proving who you are is a waste of emotional energy. In any situation, your intention is what matters. Accept another's perception of you even if it's flawed because they will eventually be shown the truth. If your heart is in the right place, then be proud and know that you're on the right path.

Never fear being different from those around you.
Never feel the need to please.
That is not a place of power.

A person's view and way of being are personal choices. They are based on a person's individual perception of reality. Their journey is theirs, just as yours is yours. Everyone has a story, and no two are the same.

When you try to defend or prove yourself, you are reacting in an ego-driven, self-absorbed way. Who are you trying to convince, them or yourself? You can't make people understand you. They are perceiving through their specific reality. Maybe you don't understand them either. So what? Does it matter? Why does someone else's opinion matter so much to you? I guarantee that your opinion doesn't matter to them!

There are plenty of people in this world who
vibrate the same as you do.
Focus on them and let the others go.

Perceptions of reality are just different. Like and love yourself and know that anybody who doesn't "get" you is missing out on a great person.

Mostly, all people want is to be validated, but you have to validate yourself first. If you depend on others to validate you, your expectations will never be met, and you will always be disappointed. It is not someone else's job or path to make you feel worthy by giving you their approval. If that's what you require, then you'll never be satisfied or happy. Happiness comes from within. It's true. Your happiness is not the responsibility of others. It is yours and yours alone.

Children need validation, and if you didn't receive validation as a child, then unfortunately you've probably carried self-worth issues into adulthood. If so, it is crucial to reach out and get the help you need to deal with these issues and feel confident in who you are. You are strong, so don't blame others or make excuses; just own your issues and take control.

3.   CHOOSING ACCEPTANCE OR JUDGMENT

Some people like being complacent. They prefer that things stay the same even if they're miserable. They don't want to change, grow, or do what's best for them. You can't do anything about that. You can explain to them how growth is necessary, but you cannot understand the issues for them. They have to want help and be willing to do the work.

God helps those who help themselves. All you can do is send others love and be a positive example. Offer encouragement and support. Listen. Give advice if you're asked for it.

No one is a finished product. We are all works in progress at different stages of development.

We must accept whatever stage others are in, as well as ourselves, without judgment. Who are we to say what another soul should be doing or not doing, learning or not learning?

JUST KEEP IN MIND THAT EACH OF US IS DOING THE BEST WE CAN AT ANY GIVEN MOMENT,

which may be way below another person's standards and may even be self-destructive, but a person will never change until they are ready to live a better life. We must all choose what is right for us in each moment. This is free will. Respect the choices of others even if you don't understand them.

Ultimately, all that each human being can do on this earth school to positively transform their own lives, the lives of those around them, and the collective as a whole is to, in the words of Mahatma Gandhi,

"Be the change you wish to see in the world."

LET'S TAKE ACTION! WORKSHEET:

Do you allow others to walk on their own path?
Do you often want to take on the burden of others?
Do you look to other people for validation?
Do you ever give away your power?
Do you find yourself accepting or judging?

Use the space below to answer and reflect:

_____

_____

_____

_____

_____

_____

_____

_____

_____

_____

_____

_____

_____

_____

_____

_____

_____

_____

_____

_____

"Happiness is not
something ready made.
It comes from your
own actions."

- Dalai Lama

CHAPTER 2

Taking Charge
of Your Own
Happiness

Life Script #6

Everyday Leadership
For Your Own Happiness

Everyday *Leadership*
For Your Own Happiness

———— • • • ————

In the world today, there is a great yearning for hope and inspiration, a yearning for leaders. I'm not referring to leaders who "run the show" and "call the shots," but those willing to lead by setting an example. That is the new leadership.

If you'd like to be a leader every day of your life, not by being elected to such a position, writing legislation, or speaking from a platform but just by being you, then consider these steps to becoming a true leader of humanity and changing the world:

1. DAILY, CHOOSE WHAT TYPE OF PERSON YOU WISH TO BE

This first step sets the tone for your entire way of life.

What kind of person have you always wanted to be?

Kind, loving, generous, supportive, spiritual, courageous, abundant? How would this person carry themselves? How would they talk? Interact with others? React to situations? Do their work?

Ask yourself,

"What am I radiating about myself?"

What is my body language: chest out, shoulders back, head high, open? Or, shrinking, hunched over, head down, shut down? Am I breathing deep and slow or shallow and fast? Observe yourself for a moment and recognize the differences.

Notice the way you are, because it affects other people. You share energy with those around you. If you wish to be a peaceful, joyful person, are you transferring thoughts of laughter and harmony or anger and separation? Do you radiate inner peace or inner struggle? Let yourself open up to who you truly want to be and the direction of your life.

2. DARE TO FEEL GOOD EVERY SINGLE DAY OF YOUR LIFE

Care about how you feel, and choose to embrace life in ways that feel good. When you nurture yourself and do the things that make you happy, you allow the light within to flow forth in expanded and amplified ways. And feeling good makes those around you feel good too.

Be less willing to feel less than good. Be more attentive to the way you feel, and more urgently attend to your vibration when you realize you're "off." By thinking happy thoughts and choosing to feel good, you demonstrate a particular way of living that allows others to believe they can live that way.

In your joy, you're demonstrating what's possible with ease and grace, and what the world needs now is evidence of what's possible. In this way, you pave the way for more joy, not only for yourself but for others, because it empowers them to see their potential.

Each of us empowers the other to the greatest degree when we are fulfilled.

3. RECOGNIZE THAT YOU ARE YOUR SOUL IN FORM

Your soul has a plan for your everyday life. See yourself as the soul that you are. Make a connection with your unlimited, infinite essence, and from there, examine the world around you.

When your view of yourself is different, your view of the world is different.

The need to control the outcome of everything fades away, and in its place is a broader perspective of quiet observance and acceptance.

From this place of loving energy, your essence desires to bring about a transition from that which has been, from old fear-based energies to a new era.

*Imagine that you are truly open
and have no fear,
that you dare to follow
your deepest inspiration,
and others will be influenced
to follow in your footsteps.*

As you begin living according to your deepest desires, you make it easier for others to do the same. You then become a living example that following your dreams can be done, that it is possible.

Maybe when you were a child it didn't feel safe to be who you really were inside: innocent, trusting, and filled with the light of love.

However, it is now safe to let your light shine.

When you permit your soul to show itself, you naturally become a loving presence. You don't have to say a word. Your energy alone will have a transforming effect and bless the world.

To be a great leader, you do not have to wait until you've reached a kind of perfection, which doesn't actually exist. It's about getting up every day and taking a step forward to share how amazing you are with the world. Being a leader is not about having control or power over others but about being a beacon of hope, inspiration, support, and encouragement. It's about being a conduit for your soul's energy in order to empower your fellow human beings to connect with their own beautiful, unique souls. This is what being a leader is truly all about.

"One person must choose a new way of being and live that difference in the presence of others so that it can be witnessed and sealed into the pattern. In doing so, we upgrade our programs of belief and send consciousness the blueprint for a new reality."

—Gregg Braden, The Divine Matrix

LET'S TAKE ACTION! WORKSHEET:

What Am I Radiating?

Ask yourself, "What am I radiating about myself this very minute?"

What is my body language? (Chest out, shoulders back, head high, open? Or, shrinking, hunched over, head down, shut down? Am I breathing deep and slow or shallow and fast? Do I radiate inner peace or inner struggle?)

Observe yourself for a moment and write it down below:

_____

_____

_____

What could I change physically about my body language to radiate more positivity?   Write it down below:

_____

_____

_____

We learned that by choosing to feel good, you demonstrate a particular way of living that allows others to believe they can live that way. What are some negative thoughts you can replace with more positive, happy ones?

Negative Thought:	The Happy Thought you'll choose instead:
1.	1.
2.	2.
3.	3.

Keep it up: Let yourself open up to who you truly want to be and the positive direction of your life.

Life
Script

#7

The
Waterfall
Effect

The  Effect

Waterfalls are beautiful and peaceful, yet their presence is so powerful that they literally alter the shape of the landscape. Human waterfalls possess that same energy.

*Simply by being,
we have the ability to change
the environment in which we find ourselves.*

Human waterfalls shape our landscape through the way they lead their lives. When someone is a waterfall for you, teaching and inspiring you by their example, by their very presence, you become the waterfall for others, and so on.

The following characteristics of waterfalls are here as a metaphor, showing how we relate to our own lives and to the lives of those we influence when they are touched by our spray.

Which type of waterfall can you be? Possibly all three?

1. THE PEACEFUL WATERFALL

Just as a waterfall in nature may form across a fault, crack, or other disruption in the earth's surface, human waterfalls can be created from chaotic situations through times that are difficult and challenging.

When others feel broken in spirit, the peaceful human waterfall overflows with unconditional love. They reserve judgment and calmly smooth the rocky edges by listening, understanding, and forgiving. Words may even be unnecessary, as their positive energy spills onto others effortlessly, changing the overall mood of the environment and those in it. In this way, people who have been affected by this type of waterfall learn to react from a place of compassion.

2. THE UNIQUE WATERFALL

Waterfalls are unique and carve out paths. No two are the same, just as

No two paths in life, no two situations, and no two people are exactly the same.

Those who have gone before you, your human waterfalls, have laid a path for you, helping you to be all that you are, eroding obstacles in your way. Some may have been huge waterfalls that have given way to many smaller ones. Or perhaps a smaller waterfall has profoundly touched only you, creating only one other waterfall directly.

Either way, the unique human waterfall inspires dreamers, original thinkers, inventors, visionaries, artists, writers, philosophers, and risk-takers viewed as crazy by some and positively brilliant by others!

3. THE POWERFUL WATERFALL

The force of nature can be powerful beyond measure, and the sheer intensity of water washing over the surface of the earth is a force to be reckoned with.

The powerful human waterfall exhibits such strength of character that it garners the trust and faith of others. These individuals are the great leaders of mankind.

Their beautiful yet strong words, messages of hope, kindness, and confident determination cascade over those who listen, motivating them to pursue the goal of serving others and taking the lead in making the world a more cooperative, safer, healthier environment in which to live and prosper.

*In every situation,
we are all given the chance to
be an evolver,
a waterfall.*

In other words, we are constantly given the opportunity to be someone who helps bring humanity into alignment with a new and positive outlook by flowing forth that energy to others.

So be a waterfall for others. Always keep in mind that your influence in the world can be beautiful, powerful, and life-changing, because when your spray reaches another, you give them the capability to shapeshift and become a waterfall too.

 **LET'S TAKE ACTION! WORKSHEET:**

Waterfall Type

Which type of waterfall are you? Possibly all three? What else can you do in your life to be a waterfall to others? Who has been a waterfall in your life and in what way? How did having them pave the way before you positively affect you?

Life
Script
#8

Do you Really Know
What *joy* is?

Do you Really Know
What *joy* is?

Why is it that all we really want and search for in life is happiness, and at the very same time, it is the one thing that eludes us the most? We all have different ideas of what would give us a feeling of happiness and joy, but there must be some common ground that we're missing. Maybe it's that most of us don't truly understand what joy is or how to attain it?

Personally, I have found what constitutes joy for me (and what does not) and how I believe each and every one of us can reach it.

1. WHAT JOY IS NOT

In most people's minds, joy is synonymous with pleasure. However, joy is not pleasure. Pleasure is a rather short-term, short-lived emotion. It appears in flashes, coming and going fairly quickly.

Joy cannot be bought or sought externally and does not give instant gratification.

Joy is also not contentment. Many of us think we've come to a place of joy when we feel momentary peace or simply a lack of trauma-drama in our lives.

Yet merely settling for a life that is "good enough" or "okay" is not joyous.

Pleasure and contentment can also bring their opposites: displeasure and discontentment. These are fleeting and complacent emotions which, unfortunately, we confuse with joy much of the time.

2. WHAT JOY IS

Joy, on the other hand, has no opposite. When we are going through pain, joy remains after pleasure and contentment are long gone.

It is a state of being that powerfully affects the world around us. Whether it's your work, family, health, etc., joy touches all that you are a part of.

Joy is a sustained, elevated, superfast vibrating energy that most people are not at all used to. A state of true joy reveals an eagerness and enthusiasm for life that many dear souls may have never felt before.

3. HOW TO FIND JOY

To live in a place of joy, one must build and grow their capacity for intense, sustained, positive energy. There are many ways to do this.

Slow down

Slow down. When we rush around, we lower our vibration, which has a negative effect on what we're doing. The more you rush, the less you will accomplish. So breathe, be calm, experience each moment, and focus on one thing at a time.

Be grateful

Be grateful. Gratitude and appreciation for all that you have in your life will raise your vibration in an ongoing fashion and keep it there. Let go of all the distractions in life in favor of those things that matter most. Simplicity will unveil the hidden joy in your life.

Be of service

Be of service. Focusing on helping others is an extremely effective way to bring joy into your life. Whether your kindness and compassion are directed toward a loved one or a stranger, a connection is made on a fundamental level. When you radiate love and help bring joy to another, you become open to the love and joy that YOU deserve.

Live the life you are capable of.

Make the time to do whatever it is that you love doing and are passionate about.

Take responsibility for your joy by creating it. Don't settle for a life that's "good enough."

Live life to the fullest.

Make it count!

If someone were to ask me what I think the meaning of life is, I would have to say bringing joy to yourself and others.

Joy is that feeling of positive intensity that exceeds all boundaries and resides inside every one of us. It does not come from a store or drift in and out of our lives from day to day. It is who we are at our core.

So do your best to simplify, savor, and always reach for a higher vibration. In this way, you will be sure to transform your search for happiness into everlasting joy.

LET'S TAKE ACTION! WORKSHEET:

Joyful Pop Quiz!

Joy and happiness are such important topics, so let's do a JOYful quiz to help this "prescription" work for you! Fill in the below remembering what you just read. If you get stumped, don't worry – just re-visit the previous pages for the answers.

What are some things that joy is NOT?

_____

_____

_____

What IS joy?

_____

_____

_____

What's the difference between joy and pleasure?

_____

_____

_____

What are the 3 ways to find joy?

1. _____

2. _____

3. _____

Keep it up: Over the next few days, think about ways you can add more TRUE joy into your life and the lives of others

Life Script #9

How to Follow Your
Dreams

How to Follow Your *Dreams*

———— • • • ————

You have, like no other person on this planet, certain contributions to offer this generation. Make no mistake about it, you are here at this particular time because the world needs you now.

More than likely, if you are reading this, your inner guidance system has been nudging you, beckoning you to move forward in a way that honors your True self.

You are the only expert on you. Therefore, it is you who must make a solid declaration as to who you are and how you wish to express yourself.

Many will say that they are afraid to do what they love to do, or that they don't have the time. I don't believe that.

You are more capable and incredible than you give yourself credit for.

Never be afraid to follow your dream no matter how "out there" it may appear to others.

Do you think people rolled their eyes at all of the inventors, visionaries, artists, and musicians who have drastically changed our lives for the better? Of course they did! But those same folks can't deny the fact that it is the dreamers who are the harbingers of positive change in the world. So if somebody doesn't support or understand your dream, just smile and think,

"Don't believe me? Just watch!"

Some people insist that the "rules of success" are very black and white. I disagree. I believe there is a HUGE grey area, and following "the rules" may not be the best way to get you where you want to go.

Your dream can be a simple one. It might be very complicated. Either way,

I want to encourage and support any dream that you may have even if no one else does.

The bottom line is the world is waiting for your dream to manifest.

Let's take a look at what I think are the truly important elements to consider when following your dream:

1. PERFECTION OR ENTHUSIASM

You can strive for perfection, but one person's interpretation of perfection is always different from another's, so who's to say what perfection is?

In fact, I believe our imperfections are what make us special.

You can be the most brilliant, talented person in the world, but if you lack the enthusiasm, passion, and excitement for what you do, then it doesn't matter how good you are. You may not be the best at what you do, but if you have great enthusiasm, which brings with it the certainty that there can be no other outcome but success, you will reach your goal, whereas others who are more skilled may not.

Enthusiasm manifests dreams. Perfection does not.

2. PRACTICALITY OR HOPE

When you have a big dream for your life, people like to tell you that you aren't being practical or that you need to be realistic. However, you do not need to know the details of how your dream will manifest. I think that

When it comes to having a dream, practicality and realism should take a back seat. These are simply limitations that we have placed upon ourselves.

And when we experience a challenge, it is not an obstacle or detour, it is part of the path itself. Otherwise, it would not be there.

Every step you take is one step closer to your dream becoming a reality. The important ingredient for realizing your dream is hope.

Hope is believing in yourself and the power of possibility. It can change the world.

Hope manifests dreams. Practicality does not.

3. KNOWLEDGE OR FEELINGS

It is extremely important to get a good education. Knowledge is a gift you give to yourself as well as to others. It allows for greater fulfillment in one's life. However, knowledge must go hand in hand with our feelings. We cannot judge our circumstances based solely on our mind's perspective.

Listening to your heart is a necessary component of following your dreams. The heart holds wisdom, as does the intellectual mind. Even when our dreams don't seem logical, our hearts can feel that they are right.

At that point, the mind must follow the direction of the heart. Let your heart set the course.

Feelings manifest dreams.
Knowledge alone does not.

So consider this a call to action.
You are one of a kind.
You have unique abilities.

And the fact of the matter is, just one person can change the world. Follow your dreams with confidence. Never give up or get discouraged, because only after you have reached your destination and looked back can you clearly see the journey you have taken. That's when you will understand all the steps that led you there and that every single one of those steps was orchestrated better than you could have ever imagined.

And when you do find your passions and share them with others, you give others permission to do the same and to realize that everyone is important in a unique way.

LET'S TAKE ACTION! WORKSHEET:

Let's Manifest Your Dreams!

What are your initial thoughts, feelings or reflections about following your dreams after reading this chapter?

_____

_____

_____

Since hope manifests dreams and practicality does not, what would your dreams look like if no "practical" obstacles were standing in your way? What would you do if you were guaranteed you would NOT fail?!

_____

_____

_____

_____

_____

_____

_____

_____

_____

Keep it up: What baby step can you take TODAY towards the dreams you just wrote down? Schedule that one task into your planner and make it happen! Then think about the next baby step and schedule that one into your planner....then keep repeating!

Life
Script
#10

Can Being *Humble* Ironically Make You a Powerful Leader?

Can Being *Humble* Ironically Make You a Powerful Leader?

———— • • • ————

Can being humble make you a powerful leader? I believe the answer to this question is a resounding "yes!" But most people in positions of power tend to allow their egos to get the best of them,

*and everyone knows
The ego does not like to be humble.*

It likes to toot its own horn. It lives to impress people and receive recognition.

We may think that our egos give us confidence, but the irony is that when one is truly and sincerely confident, all it takes is his or her presence alone to be deeply felt by others, and that is when one is the most impressive and recognized.

When a person is constantly telling us how great they are, don't you get the impression that they must feel so unimportant inside? It's sad. They need attention in order to feel good about themselves.

Those who don't need the attention and don't go looking for it are the ones who sit back while other people praise, admire, and reward them for their deeds. They are the people who inspire and command the attention of others without saying a word. Their silent presence is an invisible force of powerful, positive energy that causes them to stand out.

They are tuned in to a higher source of wisdom, and they exude gratitude for their gifts and experiences. They are aware of their talents and accomplishments, but they don't need to broadcast them because they know that others will probably find out eventually, and if they don't, that's okay, too.

Genuine humility is this combination of awareness, modesty, gratitude, and compassion for other human beings. It is a marriage between grace and fortitude,

and therein lies its power.

So how can we be humbler and recognize when our egos are making us look small? Here is a list of ten questions to ask yourself in order to keep an eye on your ego, gain some humility, and maybe even become an example of greatness to others:

1) During a conversation, are you doing most of the talking or most of the listening?

2) Does it make you feel important to talk about how much you have, especially knowing that those you're speaking to have less than you?

3) Do you tell people every time you've done something nice for someone else?

4) Can you listen to someone's story without "one-upping" them with a better one of your own?

5) Do you need to be right?

6) Are you a "name-dropper?"

7) Can you "label" individuals just by looking at them?

8) Do you place yourself on a certain level above others?

9) Are you sometimes unkind?

10) Is getting attention important to you?

If you answered yes to any of these questions, a touch of humility will more than likely serve you well. For if you are looking to feel powerful and important, the real power lies within you, not in your accomplishments, and not in your net worth.

Ironically, being humble is what gets you noticed.

It is possible to be a leader, to excel, and to be humble at the same time. When your heart is humble, you know that you are appreciated, and that is enough. You don't need a fancy title, gold star, or parade. Your humility makes you "shiny" and lets people know that you believe in yourself, which in turn gives them permission to believe in themselves. And what is more important and powerful than that?

LET'S TAKE ACTION! WORKSHEET:

Attributes of Humility
- Check List Challenge -

Below is a check list of ten questions to ask yourself in order to keep your ego in check, gain some humility, and maybe even become a positive example to others:

Check the box next to each one to see where you fit on the humility scale:

✓ Check the ♡ box for "No"

✓ Check the ⚠ box If you're working on it

	No	I'm working on it!
1) During a conversation, are you doing most of the talking?	♡	⚠
2) Does it make you feel important to talk about how much you have, especially knowing that those you're speaking to have less than you?	♡	⚠
3) Do you tell people every time you've done something nice for someone else?	♡	⚠
4) Can you listen to someone's story without "one-upping" them with a better one of your own?	♡	⚠
5) Do you need to be right?	♡	⚠
6) Are you a "name-dropper?"	♡	⚠
7) Can you "label" individuals just by looking at them?	♡	⚠
8) Do you place yourself on a certain level above others?	♡	⚠
9) Are you sometimes unkind?	♡	⚠
10) Is getting attention important to you?	♡	⚠

How to Start Over:

Take a Cue From

Mother Nature

How to Start Over:
Take a Cue From *Mother Nature*

Every spring, Mother Nature gives herself a new life. She starts over. Flowers and trees don't remember the winters of their lives. They don't focus their attention on the cold, harsh conditions that made them go into hiding. No.

All of nature begins anew in the spring. Wouldn't it feel wonderful to do the same? Completely start over?

But you don't have to wait until spring - play Mother Nature and give yourself the freedom to treat your work, relationships, and interests with a freshness and enthusiasm that pays no mind to what has gone before.

Here's how:

1. WORK

Whether you work inside the home or outside, burnout can be a definite hazard. When you become drained and exhausted, it is because your life is totally out of balance. All work and no play is a recipe for depression, anxiety, and stress.

Fun and laughter have to be a priority in your life just like anything else. Think of it as an integral part of your job because it is crucial to a life of success and prosperity. You have to make a serious commitment to being silly and goofing off because if you don't, you are of no real help to anyone, least of all yourself.

2. RELATIONSHIPS

Make a wide-eyed assessment of all your relationships.

Is your connection with your spouse or significant other on a shaky foundation of past resentments and mistakes? Have your kids or parents made you feel less than important? Did you get taken advantage of at work or do you sometimes wish your coworkers would quit making things so difficult?

Here's the thing,

The most important relationship you will ever have is with yourself.

You have to be first and foremost in importance in your life. Otherwise, you'll end up falling victim to the fleeting opinions and actions of everybody around you. That is no way to live.

So approach all of your relationships with a clean slate. It feels really good. Take your power back, make a command decision, and choose the types of relationships you want to experience. I've decided that I'm going to feel "in love," confident that I have no battles to wage.

Flowers do not fight to be the perfect expression of beauty and life that they are. They just are. So are you.

3. INTERESTS

We all have distinct interests. Pay attention to them. Take full advantage of any inner stirrings that you're experiencing at this point in your life. Let them bubble up to the surface and take root.

If you feel deeply passionate about something, then guess what – it's probably the reason you're on this planet.

Don't let another "spring" go by without taking a leap of faith and loving yourself enough to do those things that make you happy.

Start doing things that you feel are fun and exciting and fulfilling. This is your life. You do what you like, and other people can do what they like.

Do this exercise: Fast forward and imagine yourself in your eighties or nineties. Look back at your life. Did you accomplish everything you wanted to, or did you miscalculate how much time you'd have to do those things?

Quit dwelling in the past and on petty things. Get crackin' with a fresh start. Don't waste one more minute.

The bottom line is you have to break the energy that's producing a life experience that you don't want in order to allow fresh energy for a happier result. Change gears. Change perspective.

Change is good!

Without taking a lesson from the quintessential example of change, Mother Nature, we would never grow and become all that we were meant to be.

There has never been and never will be another you. Give yourself the power to bloom and stand tall as the brand new, one and only, amazing you.

LET'S TAKE ACTION! WORKSHEET:

Change is Good!

Close your eyes for a minute...fast forward and imagine yourself in your eighties or nineties, looking back at your life. Did you accomplish everything you wanted to, or did you miscalculate how much time you'd have to do those things? Open your eyes and reflect on how that made you feel and what changes you can make to now give yourself the power to bloom:

_____
_____
_____
_____
_____
_____

What changes would you like to make so that when you are in your eighties or nineties, you can look back and say you accomplished everything you wanted? For example:

1) Work:

_____
_____

2) Relationships:

_____
_____

3) Interests:

_____
_____

"If you change
the way you look at things,
the things you look at
change."

-Wayne Dyer

CHAPTER 3

Harnessing the Law of *Attraction*

Life Script #12

Is There a Formula
for Making the
Law of Attraction
Work for You?

(You B+E=T!)

Is There a Formula for Making the Law of *Attraction* Work for You?

You B+E=T!

———— • • • ————

Belief + Expectation = Truth

If you were given the key to unlock and access anything in life, would you use it?

Unconsciously, we are constantly opening ourselves to life circumstances, both good ones and bad ones.

But what if we could deliberately create them?

That would be absolutely amazing, wouldn't it? But by being complacent about the all-encompassing law of attraction, we unwittingly allow experiences into our lives, experiences that make us unhappy and hold us back.

Just like The Law of Gravity, we may not see it or understand how it works,

but the minute we forget it's there, we fall and hit the ground! However, our lives don't have to play out "randomly" or be a constant uphill battle.

I'm sure you've noticed that some people seem to lead charmed lives. They make it look effortless, but I'm willing to "BET" they use a particular strategy: Belief + Expectation = Truth, whether they realize it or not. It is a rather short, straightforward equation, yet the ease or difficulty with which it is calculated into your own life is entirely up to you.

Let's breakdown this formula so you can start recalculating life in your favor:

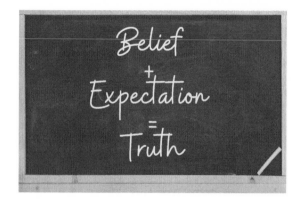

1. WHAT YOU BELIEVE

Belief.

Your beliefs are simply thoughts that you keep thinking over and over and over again. Eventually, you believe them to be true.

But I ask you, are those repeated thoughts actually true?

Is this a belief of yours because your parents believe it, or your friends agree with it, or because you hear it on the news every evening?

Does this belief feel good or bad? Does it uplift or depress you?

Your belief system is the foundation of your entire life. Wouldn't you enjoy a better life if you believed you could?

Take some time right now to think about what you believe and why. This activity alone causes a shift in energy that can turn negative ideas into positive ones.

When you have an ongoing negative thought, which has or will become a belief, question it!

Do you believe you can own a beautiful home? If not, why?

Is it because you've been conditioned to think you don't deserve it, or because the news is telling you that the economy is bad?

Here is the issue: External forces that you cannot control are controlling you.

So forget about what is going on outside of you. Focusing on external circumstances only creates excuses and blame, which are never in alignment with those things that make us happy. If we train our brains to regularly think about and feel the positive aspects of life, that higher, happier energy frequency will be a vibrational match to the abundance we desire.

The law of attraction is a universal force that is always working, whether we are aware it is or not, and it never yields anything other than what our vibrational frequency inspires. We're constantly receiving from the law of attraction and asking for what we desire with our vibration, so why not get what we want?

Begin taking the negative beliefs that you hold and flipping them to their positive opposites. Think those new, positive thoughts over and over and over again until they become your dominant beliefs. This may take awhile. As I mentioned, the B + E = T equation can be easy or difficult for you depending on your willingness to let go of the negative beliefs you have about yourself and the world around you.

You must be sure, though, to approach this exercise with kindness and compassion for yourself.

If you do, you'll raise your vibration to the level of that which you seek. If you beat yourself up about your thinking and become angry or frustrated, or let yourself become exhausted and depleted from stress or lack of rest, that which you seek will always elude you. You will unintentionally become vulnerable to circumstances of the lower vibrational frequencies, which the law of attraction will have to bring you instead.

Choose your beliefs based on how they make you feel, not on "fact." Think about perfect health, prosperity, peace, and so on. If this is hard for you and feels more like denial, then do not place these thoughts within the context of the current circumstances of your life. You won't be a vibrational match to something you're too aware you don't have.

Don't think of the "hows": How am I going to have a beautiful home or how am I going to find a career that I love? Simply think of the good things in life as positive concepts all on their own.

The emotional connection you make with these ideas, without figuring out how they fit into your current situation, will activate them in your vibration and begin the process of allowing the law of attraction to do its job in a positive way for you.

That brings us to step two because what you believe is . . .

2. WHAT YOU CAN EXPECT

Expectation.

When your mind has given its attention to a thought long enough that it has become a belief, and has accepted without a doubt that it will transpire, then an expectation has been created. You know for a fact that whatever you believe will eventually occur. You are focusing on it without resistance. There is a knowing inside of you that it must be coming, and therefore, you're looking for it. This leads us to the final step because your expectation of "it" . . .

3. MAKES IT TRUE

Truth.

Maintaining the vibration of a certain belief, and thus a certain expectation, allows the law of attraction to guide it into alignment with you and make it your truth. The Universe must show you the evidence of that which is active in your vibration. You have included "it" in your vibration. This can, indeed, work for you or against you.

The crux of our inability to create in our lives is the self-defeating belief that we cannot have, be, or do that particular thing that we want so badly. For then we certainly will not expect to have, be, or do that thing, and therefore it will never be true.

However, it is so hard to fool yourself by saying, for example, "I believe I own a new car," when you know damned well you don't. Therefore, think of whatever you are wanting to have as existing out there in the realm of all possible worlds.

☑ If it's out there somewhere, then could it be possible . . . ever?

☑ Has it happened before?

☑ Have you seen it or heard of it happening to someone else?

☑ Then maybe, just maybe, you can expect it to happen again.

And so it's true that it is likely to happen. You don't know when, where, or how. All you need to know is the possibility of it.

NOW USE THE EQUATION:
BELIEF + EXPECTATION = TRUTH

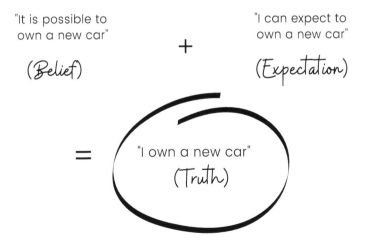

"It is possible to own a new car"

(Belief)

+

"I can expect to own a new car"

(Expectation)

=

"I own a new car"

(Truth)

See how that works? With practice, this can become easier and you'll feel the universe flowing with you, instead of against you, in no time!

Bring your focus and attention inward and realize that anything is possible. The only thing holding us back is our repetitive thoughts of doubt and negativity which, with some determination, can completely turn around into repetitive thoughts of possibility, in which we have sole creative control.

Try it. Experiment with it. Use your imagination. Repeat that belief of possibility over and over again until you can expect it. You'll be amazed at your deliberate creations!

LET'S TAKE ACTION! WORKSHEET:

Let's Practice!

What is a negative belief you currently hold to be true?

....

....

What's the opposite, positive version of that belief?

....

....

The above will replace your negative belief and will be your NEW, positive belief! Now it's time to fill in you B + E = T formula below!

Your new belief: Your new expectation:

....   **+**   ....

....

=   Your new Truth:

....

....

Now try it with another negative belief:

What is a negative belief you currently hold to be true?

....

....

What's the opposite, positive version of that belief?

....

....

The above will replace your negative belief and will be your NEW, positive belief! Now it's time to fill in you B + E = T **formula below!**

Your new belief: Your new expectation:

....   **+**   ....

....

=

Your new Truth:

....

....

Amazing work!

Repeat the above formula with as many negative beliefs as you can. Then be sure to revisit this page often to reinforce your new, positive beliefs!

And remember B + E = T!

Life
Script
℞ **#13**

How to Create *Abundance* Every Day

How to Create
Abundance Every Day

The fact is that we create abundance for ourselves every single day. How can that be, you ask? You may be saying to yourself, "I don't have abundance. I never have any money. I have all these aches and pains, and my significant other is probably going to leave me just like the last two did!"

Well, you are definitely creating abundance in your life, but the big question is: an abundance of what?

It is very possible to be creating an abundance of lack, an abundance of poor health, and an abundance of troubled relationships in your life. You see, we all create various things for ourselves—some good, some not so good—but the key is to recognize that sometimes we're our own worst enemies.

The exciting part is that we have the power to turn things around and become our heroes. On the road to becoming more self-aware and making positive changes that inspire the type of abundance you want in your life, ask yourself these five important questions:

1. WHAT MESSAGE AM I DELIVERING TO MYSELF?

We send lots of fun, kind, caring text messages and emails to other people, but what messages are we sending to ourselves? How about: "You aren't good enough. You don't deserve to be loved. You are unimportant. Have a nice day."

We need to start delivering love and support to ourselves. When you are constantly putting yourself down, what kind of abundance do you think you are attracting? So how about writing this note to yourself from now on: "I AM good enough. I DO deserve to be loved. I AM important. Have a nice day!"

2. AM I SURE THAT MY
MONEY CAN ONLY COME FROM ONE PLACE?

Don't get stuck in the mindset that you know where your money can come from. This limiting belief will trip you up every time by blocking any monetary abundance that is trying to come to you.

If you say to yourself, "It can't come from this, and it can't come from there. It can only come from here, and here is not looking too good," then you are deciding that for yourself.

In truth, there are infinite possibilities; you just can't see them.

People receive money from unexpected sources all the time. There isn't a finite amount. There is plenty to go around, but not if you shut down the stream before it even has a chance to flow in your direction like a current (hence, the word "currency"). You are essentially saying, "No, I cannot have the money that I need."

Therefore, your limiting beliefs are creating an abundance of lack that can only be turned around by believing differently.

3. AM I JEALOUS OF OTHER PEOPLE?

This question can be difficult for most individuals to admit. We don't like to think of ourselves as being envious of someone else, but if you've ever seen another person and made a derogatory remark about how or why they have all that they do, then you need to take note of it.

Be aware that another's wealth and happiness are not taking away from yours.

If you are critical of another person's success, no matter how much you think they don't deserve it, be VERY careful. The last thing you want to do is throw negative energy at someone lest it comes back to bite you! Just remember that the Universe has an infinite supply of everything. Instead of being jealous, say, "Good for them!"

4. DO I GET ATTENTION WHEN I HAVE CHALLENGES?

Usually, we all get more attention when other people feel bad for us because of something we're dealing with. It may be hard for some to understand why, but many people out there create the wrong kind of abundance because they like getting inappropriate attention. It may be a subconscious issue. They may not even realize that they do it.

And yes, we all want to be supportive and helpful to those who truly need it, but

There are those folks who always have something to complain about. What they are actually doing is creating an abundance of negative circumstances in their lives and reaffirming them over and over again.

These people are definitely their own worst enemies, and when we cater to their every trouble in life, we are doing a real disservice to them.

5. AM I STAGNANT?

Complacency is not a good trait to have. We cannot create positive abundance in our lives if we don't make positive changes. When you don't like the way your life is going and you do nothing to change it, then you have no right to complain when things don't get better.

We all need to recognize that our lives and our happiness are our responsibilities. Doing what you've done day after day and year after year and wondering why nothing good ever happens to you means you are "stagnant." Don't expect your life to change if you are not willing to first make an effort to change.

So now the question is: How can we all be more aware of and transform the kind of abundance we are creating each day? The answer: Love yourself. Be open to the power of possibility, live and let live, be supportive but not enabling, and make a concerted effort to be the change you wish to see.

LET'S TAKE ACTION! WORKSHEET:

Let's Create Abundance Every Day...

Now it's your turn! On the road to becoming more self-aware and making positive changes that inspire the type of abundance you want in your life, ask yourself these five important questions:

1) What message am I delivering to myself?

_____

_____

_____

2) Am I sure that my money can only come from one place?

_____

_____

_____

3) Am I jealous of other people?

_____

_____

_____

4) Do I get attention when I have challenges?

_____

_____

_____

5) Am I stagnant?

_____

_____

_____

Keep it up: What specific positive changes can you make this week to incorporate more abundance in your life?

Life
Script
📄 #14

Is It *My Turn* Yet?

Is It *My Turn* Yet?

———— • • • ————

When you feel you've done everything you can think of, have planted all the seeds necessary, but are still waiting around to reap the harvest, it's hard not to get discouraged. Here are four reasons why your dreams still haven't manifested and how you can kick them into high gear!

1. RELEASE THE FEAR

Fear of failure, success, change, and the unknown are all common emotions to experience when we try to let go of what is familiar to us. Taking a leap of faith and reaching beyond our comfort zones can create a major tug-of-war between the safety of a predictable life and complete uncertainty. We feel out of control like we're falling off a cliff, and that is a scary situation.

In order to go beyond the fear, you have to shift your perception. Figure out what you're really afraid of: your kids might feel neglected, you're not as smart or as skilled as people think you are, your friends won't understand, etc. Then stop and assess whether or not these excuses are truths. What would be much worse is realizing at the end of your life that you sacrificed fulfilling your life's purpose out of fear.

Fear has no power.
It isn't something tangible that you can hold in your hand.
Fear exists only in one's mind.

So don't put yourself in a position of regret, wondering what could have been, wondering how your life could have been different or how you might have been able to change the lives of others in some positive and profound way. Instead, choose to see your life as an exciting adventure in which you are always protected!

2. PULL THE WEEDS

You must remove the weeds in your garden to make room for flowers to grow and bloom.

The weeds I'm referring to are obstacles in the form of limiting beliefs and emotions that have to be cleared away. Every piece of baggage you've been carrying around with you, any deep-seated subconscious belief and emotion of the negative variety, needs to be dealt with.

Just like in school, there are prerequisites that need to be satisfied before you can graduate to the next level. For instance, if you are still harboring anger against someone from many years ago, even if it's yourself, that anger is blocking your abundance.

Let it go.

Forgive, in your mind, everyone who has ever hurt you.

This process is not for them; it Is for you.

This will open up a gateway connecting you to the bounty of your harvest.

In this way, as you work hard to increase your vibration, each of the issues and emotions that no longer resonate with that higher frequency must come to the surface where you can be conscious of them. At that point, they will begin to manifest in your conscious reality. These beliefs surface in layers like peeling an onion. If they surfaced all at once, we wouldn't be able to handle it.

When limiting beliefs manifest as experiences, it isn't a punishment or a setback, but an opportunity to deal with something that has been preventing you from manifesting your desires. Once you are aware of the belief, you can change the belief. Acknowledge your success and progress. Weeding is just as important as planting and watering the seeds. And keep in mind that each challenge brings you closer to your goals!

3. TRUST THE UNIVERSE

You very well may be right on the verge of realizing your dreams when doubt, worry, disappointment, and resentment set in, and you start to give up. However, things don't happen in the physical until they first manifest in the spiritual. Through thought and emotion, they take form.

Divine Timing requires patience and faith. All will take place at the exact perfect time, not a time of your choosing.

If you can learn to trust the Universe, when your dream does manifest, it will be better than you could have ever imagined!

When things look bleak and something you wanted to have happened doesn't, it's always because it wasn't a good enough or big enough vision for your life. That makes "disappointments" very exciting! It's often said that in the chaos, the angels are doing their best work. Stay positive and you'll get closer and closer.

4. GET OUT OF THE WAY

Stop trying to make things happen. Stop seeking, searching, and forcing. Get out of your own way! If you do, synchronicities will begin to occur. Perhaps a complete stranger who is an expert in your field of study will start talking to you while you're waiting in line at a store, then a friend you haven't thought of in months will call you with an opportunity. That is how it will happen. People will come out of the woodwork and find you!

It feels completely different from what you're used to experiencing.

Naturally, you stop pushing so hard and end up getting a lot more accomplished, as everything easily falls into place. You allow the chips to fall where they may, for a change.

When you feel peaceful, calm, and happy (not fearful, desperate, frantic, tired, or focused on lack), that's when things start happening! Realize that a shift in your energy of 180 degrees is required, and the way you've always done things in the past is not going to work anymore.

Quit needing to control the process and the outcome. Accept that you are not in control, and be thankful for that, because a much higher, much more powerful force is. People feel they have to control everything, but the truth is, things get done if they're supposed to get done. If something doesn't get done, or something doesn't happen, it wasn't meant to be. Everything works out for the best.

When you let life flow and unfold naturally and become open to any process and any result, life becomes much, much easier.

You can't fully understand this until you've felt and experienced how it works. Just try it and see how your life begins to change. However, you have to trust that your Higher Self, Higher Power, Universe, angels, or whomever you believe in knows more than you do and can make things happen for you a whole lot easier, faster, and better than you ever could in your three-dimensional, physical body.

Don't assume that things take a long time to manifest, either, as this belief will also delay the materialization of your dreams. If you feel like you've been waiting around forever, and life doesn't seem to be going the way you had hoped, stop and consider whether you are doing all you can to be open to the power of possibility. Acknowledge that none of us can foresee the endless combinations of ways in which our lives will unfold. Let go of the "only way this could happen" theory, feel centered knowing that you are loved and that peace is everywhere, and make room for unexpected, exciting, unimaginable events to present themselves to you with light speed!

LET'S TAKE ACTION! WORKSHEET:

Let's Make Our Dreams Manifest!

1) In what aspects of your life do you need to release the fear?

2) Where in your life do you need to pull the weeds and let go?

3) What obstacles are you facing right now with feelings of fear, desperation or lack that need to be replaced with feelings of peace, calm, and happiness instead?

4) What outcome should you stop trying to control?

Keep it up: Now cross out all the SHOULD's and NEED TO's in the above questions and instead write you WILL next to them!

Read them out loud to yourself every morning!

Life Script #15

Start *Manifesting* What You <u>Do</u> Want and Stop Manifesting What You <u>Don't</u>

Start Manifesting What You <u>Do</u> Want and Stop Manifesting What You <u>Don't</u>

———— • • ————

If you are thinking or speaking, you are manifesting.

It doesn't matter to the Universe whether those thoughts and words are negative or positive. It will be supportive of whatever you "want" and make it a part of your life.

For instance, if Jim says, "My business is struggling. I have no orders coming in," day after day, Jim has essentially programmed his subconscious mind to believe that this is the way things are. The Universe receives this as an affirmation that Jim is making about his life. Apparently, this is what Jim wants to create with his free will because he's giving it so much energy. So the Universe says, "Okay, Jim's business is struggling, and he has no orders coming in. Done."

Sally might be trying to lose weight, but she looks in the mirror every morning and thinks, "I am so fat!" Again, "Okay, Sally, you can have what you want. You are so fat! Done."

When you constantly connect to a belief you have about your life, The Universe will bring more and more of whatever that is to you.

Here's the challenge: We don't even realize that we are creating the negative experiences we are having and blocking or delaying the success and abundance that we are meant to enjoy. How do we edit our thoughts and words so we quit sabotaging ourselves, and instead, open the doors to happiness?

1. FOCUS YOUR ATTENTION ON THE GOOD

Don't focus on what's wrong; focus on what's right.

If you are placing your energy and attention on something negative, you are attracting more of exactly what you don't want.

What you need to do is attract the opposite of what you currently have. So since what you see is what you are going to believe as you move forward, see yourself as healthy. See yourself as strong. See yourself as accomplishing your dreams. There is huge power in the vision you have of yourself. If your vision is limited, your life will be limited. Shift your focus from what you think you are to what you can become. Put energy into that. If your vision is negative, your life will follow.

2. CATCH YOURSELF

So how do you catch yourself when being negative? And how do you turn it into being positive? It's very easy to just say, "Be positive and everything will be okay!" But we are human beings, not robots. So first, create a built-in warning system that will identify negative thoughts, allowing you a chance to choose a better way.

Start listening to your thoughts, and ask yourself the following questions as a negativity checklist:

- Is the thought self-defeating?
- Is it critical of yourself or others?
- Does it encourage excess worry?
- Is the thought hard to get rid of?
- Does thinking it make you upset or sad?
- Are you sure this is the way you want things to turn out?

Once you recognize that you are broadcasting negative thoughts and words out into the Universe, you can turn it around by deciding not to. Say to yourself, "Delete!" and replace it with something positive. You soon will discover just how many life-defeating proclamations you've been putting out there. The Universe will quickly respond to this change of direction.

3. SAY THANK YOU: EMBRACE CHALLENGES AND BE GRATEFUL

Say "thank you," no matter what. "Thank you" is one of the most powerful phrases you can send out into the Universe! Thank your past no matter how painful it was. You don't need to know why things happened the way they did. You need to be thankful that you got through them and learned whatever it was your soul was meant to learn through the process of your life. Accept that things couldn't have been any other way.

Gratitude is a force that, when unleashed, turns everything into a good experience. Yes, everything. There is always a life lesson to be learned, a challenge to experience, or an opportunity for growth. If you view a situation from that perspective, nothing is ever bad—nothing. The reason is quite simple.

When we develop an attitude of gratitude, that which is negative ceases to exist.

Thanking everything that is in your life, including the negatives, may seem ridiculous at first, but here's the magic:

When you thank something negative for happening or thank a negative thought for being there, you've just negated the negative and turned it into positive energy!

At this point, miracles start to happen!

*The more thankful you become for
everything around you,
the more abundance will flow into your life.*

*So thank everything, even when you're
not so sure you're grateful for it.
In time, you will be.*

Keep in mind that every day you are planting the seeds of tomorrow. Have a big vision for your life and plant seeds of greatness. You will not only change your life but the lives of those around you, as well. And remember to be careful what you wish for. You just might get it!

LET'S TAKE ACTION! WORKSHEET:

Start manifesting what you want

1) What positives do you want to attract into your life? Where can you shift your focus from negative to positive?

_____

_____

2) Practice using the built-in warning system below to help identify negative thoughts and allow the chance to choose better thoughts instead.

Start listening to your thoughts, and ask yourself the following questions:

<u>Circle yes or no:</u>

• Is the thought self-defeating?	Yes	No
• Is it critical of yourself or others?	Yes	No
• Does it encourage excess worry?	Yes	No
• Is the thought hard to get rid of?	Yes	No
• Does thinking it make you upset or sad?	Yes	No
• Are you sure this is the way you want things to turn out?	Yes	No

3) It's time to say "thank you" to your past, no matter how painful it was! Can you think of 3 difficult times in your life that you can now reframe and be thankful for the lesson your soul was meant to learn through the process of your life? How does that make you feel?

_____

_____

_____

_____

Life
Script
#16

Reset your *Reality* Every Day

Reset your *Reality* Every Day

People from all over the country come together in unity to witness a total solar eclipse, whether in person, on television, or over the internet. It is a rather rare occurrence and a type of reset for our country and the planet as a whole, a turning off and turning back on in much the same way we reboot our computers. What few of us realize is that we can all reset our thoughts, and hence, our realities, every single day. We don't need to wait for an extraordinary cosmic event to take place.

There are five very simple, yet very powerful words that we don't often speak or even think. The words are

"I am looking forward to . . ."

You may wonder, "How could thinking or saying these words possibly make a difference in my life?" The quick answer is that by doing so,

you are consciously creating your reality.

By playing these words over in your mind, you'll not only start to recognize how many times you catch yourself thinking negatively, but you'll also see how differently you feel and how differently your life begins to look. Be consistent, and there will be an unmistakable shift.

What are you looking forward to?

Have you asked yourself that question?

Specifically, maybe you are looking forward to your house being paid off or your children getting good grades in school. However, you could also be more general and look forward to your abundance, inner peace, or perfect health. You fill in the blank. You can be looking forward to just one thing or many things. It is completely up to you.

What do you need to be truly happy? How about, "I am looking forward to a brand-new beginning." It doesn't matter, just so it's important to you. Make it your mantra.

Fill your thoughts with these words. Replace your mind's incessant chatter with them.

This is how you create consciously, through the intentional use of your focus, as opposed to creating through the unconscious, internal noise that is usually negative.

You will find that your thoughts are much more effective in the physical world than your actions. This is because

Things happen energetically first, then they manifest physically.

Creating takes little time or effort, just awareness in the present moment. Nothing is more powerful.

By using this technique, you will be able to, once and for all, see how your thoughts are changing your life and reality. But to further understand this principle, we need to acknowledge why it works:

1. IMMEDIATELY FOCUSES ON PROGRESS

Concentrating on what you are looking forward to instantly places you in a positive, hope-filled mindset. It makes you feel like everything you want in life is within reach, that it's realistic. It also keeps you in a high vibration. There is no room for a "victim" or "lack" mentality, just appreciation and enthusiasm.

Pay close attention to your emotions because they are your guidance system. They tell you what you're doing to or with your vibrational level. They tell you when you are out of sync with what you want and who you are. You cannot have your mind focused on negative results and have positive outcomes happen in your life. If your thoughts are negative, you will experience lack. You will have feelings of victimization. Simply ask yourself, "Have I suffered enough? Is it enough already?"

Instead, by using the mantra, "I am looking forward to . . ." in your daily life, you become empowered and excited and start to believe and notice that forces are at work behind the scenes. You're able to comprehend and acknowledge that miraculous circumstances beyond your limited scope are falling into place simply for the purpose of your bliss. And you are, perhaps for the first time in your life, allowing them.

2. FULLY ANCHORS THE PRESENT MOMENT

Even though you're "looking forward," this is not necessarily something far off or in the distance. You are there and focusing on it in the present moment. It is happening, and you can't wait!

It is on the schedule. It is part of the plan. It's a done deal, and that is your point of power. The how, when, where is unimportant. The Universe will fill in the details. The bottom line is you have opened the door to infinite possible ways so what you are looking forward to will manifest.

3. DIRECTS WHAT SHOWS UP

You have the capability of directing only certain situations into your energy field and vibration. Constant thoughts of what you are looking forward to keep your mind off of the situations that would normally worry or upset you, and therefore, blocks them. Just as your thoughts can block what it is that you want, they can also block what you don't want.

What is crucial to remember is that attention to anything activates its energy in your energy field. Even if you're saying "no" to it, you're saying "yes" if you're giving it your attention. So, what are you letting in?

By changing your random thoughts to pointed thoughts of what you are looking forward to, you are choosing what shows up in your life. For something to show up, you have to acknowledge it. If you do, then that activates all of the things that resonate on that same vibrational level, and then that is what flows into your life.

Start today! Become more actively involved in the unfoldment of events in your life by calling forth your blessings right now. I am looking forward to my best life! I am looking forward to love, fun, and wealth in all ways! How about you?

LET'S TAKE ACTION! WORKSHEET:

Let's practice resetting our reality

Get into the reset mindset!

Concentrating on what you are looking forward to instantly places you in a positive, hope-filled mindset.

What are you looking forward to? Write as many things as you can think of!

_____

_____

_____

_____

_____

_____

_____

_____

_____

_____

_____

_____

_____

Life Scripts

" The practice of forgiveness is our most important contribution to the healing of the world. "

- Marianne Williamson

CHAPTER 4

Healing

Life
Script
℞ #17

What It Takes to Survive
Disappointment
and
Heartbreak

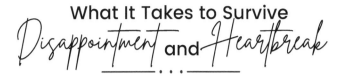

What It Takes to Survive
Disappointment and Heartbreak

We've all been there. Disappointment and heartbreak feel like being gutted inside; we are sure that we will never be happy again. Whether someone we deeply love chooses to leave us, a dear friend or family member passes away, or something that we've been striving for our entire life doesn't work out, there are a few things we can all keep in mind to help us through those trying times:

1. LEARNING, HEALING, AND COURAGE

There are certain lessons in life that no one can teach us. We must experience many situations for ourselves to better understand what it means to be human. All of life's challenges are simply opportunities for our souls to grow. Each bump in the road is just another stepping-stone being laid down along our life path, bringing us one step closer to where we need to be. In time, we heal, becoming stronger and wiser for the trial.

Remember that peace is everywhere, within every person and situation we encounter, and that the spirit can never truly be wounded and it can certainly never die.

2. TAKING CARE OF YOURSELF

When we're faced with a situation that seems unbearable, connecting to feelings of disappointment and devastation is unavoidable. The question is how long are we going to stay attached to the heartache and pain—and can we protect ourselves from becoming emotionally fragmented and get centered again?

The best thing you can do to bring comfort to yourself is this:

Before falling asleep at night,
think about something in your life
or in the world that is good.

That's it. Do not fall asleep with negative thoughts in your head, because if you do, you will only program your subconscious mind with more feelings of unhappiness. The result of feeding the brain negative information just before dozing off will ensure we wake up more and more depressed each day. If you can try to see your world as being a little brighter each night before sleep, tomorrow will look a little brighter, and so will the day after that, and the day after that, and so on.

It's okay to look behind you in the rearview mirror from time to time, but believe me, you don't want to live there.

Move forward.
Soon you will find a way to
smile, laugh, and have fun again.

Just know that changing your focus to happier thoughts will eventually make those unhappy times seem much less difficult.

3. BECOMING THE PHOENIX

In mythology, the Phoenix is a bird reborn from its own ashes. Like the Phoenix, we can observe in our own lives that

disintegration brings with it
transformation and rebirth.

What was meant to harm you will always be repurposed for your good. Whatever the circumstance, no matter how horrific it appears, *we have to know and trust that it never would have happened unless something very good and very important was going to come from it.*

Our Universe is loving, caring, and supportive—always. So in the case of a breakup with a friend or lover or the loss of a job, remember that if a person or situation is not right for you or is doing harm to you in some way, it will be taken out of your life.

Disappointment and heartbreak are always opportunities for someone or something bigger and better to arrive for you. Room needs to be made at certain times in your life for that unexpected great person or job to make its presence known. One major "upset" will take you from the lowest point in your life straight up to the pinnacle if you

just open your heart and mind to the limitless possibilities.

When we start seeing those troubling times as blessings in disguise, advantageous and essential to the next chapter of our lives, then we are better able to survive and detach from the pain and

welcome the future with open arms.

LET'S TAKE ACTION! WORKSHEET:

Let's Heal...

Next time you go through disappointment or heartbreak, ask yourself:

1) What have I learned?

_____

_____

_____

_____

_____

2 How can I take care of myself?

_____

_____

_____

_____

_____

_____

3) How can I rise like the Phoenix?

_____

_____

_____

_____

_____

Life
Script
Rx #18

Re-Parent Yourself
to Repair Yourself:
Making Your Inner Child
Happy and *Whole*

Re-Parent Yourself to Repair Yourself: Making Your Inner Child Happy and Whole

. . .

When a child experiences trauma in any form, the growth of the inner child can become stunted; it does not fully complete its growth process. As one matures physically into an adult, one's view of themselves and the world is greatly influenced by the pain of that child within that stopped growing at a particular age: Two years old? Five years old? Seven?

For instance, if as a child you were unloved or abused, then as an adult, you may manifest patterns of bad relationships that continue to repeat themselves. Or maybe you experienced poverty or felt insecure in your environment, so now, perhaps, success and stability continuously evade you.

Notice that these negative and destructive patterns are born from your inner child.

However, no matter what you may have gone through,

The good news is healing and growth of your inner child can take place now with your support.

There are three easy and fun aspects of life that everyone can focus on to more easily embrace and empower their inner child and become a happy, whole adult:

1. YOURSELF

Connect with your inner child simply by being child-like, which does not mean being child-ish. Those are two very different behaviors. The childish person is petulant, self-absorbed, demanding, irrational, obnoxious, irresponsible, etc. In contrast,

The childlike individual looks at the world through eyes of wonder.

He or she notices the beauty of nature that surrounds them, laughs at themselves and doesn't take life too seriously, and

returns to a way of being that embraces magic – a return to innocence.

Being a mature adult does not preclude one from being childlike. There is pure wisdom inherent in the qualities of a child, a pure essence that emanates. We, as adults, can retain that purity or reconnect with it, and ultimately channel our inner child. By living in that natural, original vibration, we can easily live in the moment, not worrying about the future or dwelling on the past. Instead, you realize that the concepts of age and time are irrelevant.

Every minute of the day presents an opportunity to **be unconditionally loving, nurturing, and kind to yourself.** That is truly what your inner child needs and wants and is crying out for, so why not give it?

You can be that caring parent you wish you'd had by taking great care of yourself today.

No one knows how to make you happy better than you.

Think about what would make you happy, and be that for yourself. Don't rely on someone else to do it. Get rid of limiting thoughts, because children don't see life that way. Free your thoughts and picture yourself as a small child. Honor your inner child who is always with you. Talk to her or him. Find out what they would like and what they need from you.

You have the power to heal this child's wounds. Give them whatever it is they did not receive. Do what needs to be done for this child, and your life will reflect the new happy and whole person that you can be now that you've integrated your happy and whole child within.

2. CHILDREN

Another wonderful way to heal your inner child is to be around children, either by raising your own or being a teacher or caregiver of some sort. You can be the unconditionally loving parent or mentor that you did not have for someone else. Just as you have the ability to directly love and nurture yourself, doing that for another child is a cathartic experience. Indirectly, you are loving and nurturing your inner child. You best learn by teaching others and

you best heal by healing others.

When you're around children, give them your undivided attention. Listen to them. You will begin to see the world the way they see it. Let them help you relive your childhood as a fun, positive experience. Play their games, marvel at their imagination, and follow their thought processes. **You will feel their pure vibration.**

As adults, we tend to overlook so much. We miss the details of life. A child, however, is extremely observant. They have wild imaginations.

*Their minds are expansive.
As we grow older,
we lose those qualities to a great degree.*

Being around a child will allow you to shift gears in your thinking and consider things you may have never considered. A little one's presence makes you contemplate what is important in life and that adults may have many things wrong.

3. ANIMALS

Are you an animal lover? Our pets bring out the child in us. They understand unconditional love. They nurture us, and in return, we nurture them. It is an even exchange of our energies. We can look into each other's eyes and know how the other is feeling and what they need. It's an unspoken, heart-based form of communication.

Most pet owners will tell you that their animal is also one of their children. This is because the soul of a pet shines through their being as it does in a small child.

They are beautiful, caring beings who add enormous amounts of joy to our lives. They innocently exude love just like children do.

There is no filter of anger or resentment through which they see you. They are pure love and light. Because of that, being with an animal, feeling their pure vibration, seeing the world through their innocent lens, is deeply healing to one's inner child. They give us the unconditional love, affection, and attention that we yearn for.

Our pets are always there for us. They never let us down or hurt us. We can depend on them to offer emotional support whenever we have a need.

Your inner child is an aspect of your soul.

It is the child within that follows you into adulthood. You cannot deny this part of you. If your life feels fractured, in need of repair, this is your inner child tugging on your sleeve begging you to work with it and acknowledge its importance. Honor the healing and growth of your inner child as well as the wisdom it has to share with you. You'll be amazed as your being is transformed back into its original wholeness.

LET'S TAKE ACTION! WORKSHEET:

Let's make your inner child happy!

1) What are some ways you can connect to your inner child? How can you be more child-like?

2) What is the difference between child-like and child-ish?

3) Picture yourself as a small child - what did you need or want that was never fulfilled?

Now as an adult you have the power to give your inner child the things you lacked.

In what ways can you be your own parent to your inner child now and give YOURSELF the love, comfort, support or stability you never got as a child?

Life Script #19

Learning From Tragedy

Learning From Tragedy

When a horrific tragedy befalls us, like the massacre of innocent lives, we are compelled to search our souls for answers to questions: "Why did this happen?" "How could someone do this?" "Is it possible to comprehend any trace of meaning in the wake of such a senseless act?"

I, myself, have racked my brain and delved deep into my spiritual side to try and find answers to questions like these. I hope that the thoughts I'm sharing here will help you, too, and offer food for thought as you sort through life's more trying times:

1. GOOD VS EVIL

Just as there is great good in the world, there is also immense evil, and the two sides play tug-of-war. It's a back-and-forth struggle.

Whenever "good" appears to be winning, "evil" desperately tries to knock it off balance.

However, we know that when the human spirit is faced with grave circumstances, it rallies and becomes that much stronger.

2. FREE WILL

Every individual has free will. We are each given a choice as to how we use it. You may choose to use your free will to do good or to do evil in the world. It is crucial not to waver but to take a firm stance on one side or the other. Hopefully, it's obvious which choice most of us have made.

3. VICTIMS AND SURVIVORS

Victims and the survivors of tragedy are awe-inspiring teachers of humanity.

They instill in us feelings of compassion, sympathy, and empathy. No one ever dies in vain. No one ever suffers in vain. It is the job of the rest of us to be the students and to learn as much as we possibly can from their extraordinary feats of courage. They are leading the human race toward the evolution and creation of a world that understands only love and respect for the sanctity of life itself.

Hearing stories of the many heroes is uplifting—ones who don't think twice before standing in harm's way, sacrificing their own lives so that others might live. Many survivors go on to bring peace and comfort to witnesses of other tragedies and their families. And each such survivor proves once again that good is always winning.

LET'S TAKE ACTION! WORKSHEET:

Reframing Tragedy

Can you think of a tragedy that you have learned from?

Did it make you stronger?

What other ways did it end up positively affecting you?

_____

_____

_____

_____

_____

_____

_____

_____

_____

_____

_____

_____

Life
Script
Rx #20

Forgiveness
is an Act of Strength

Forgiveness Is an Act of Strength

———— • • • ————

Many people hold the belief that forgiving a person who has hurt them is an act of weakness, that it's the same as simply letting that person get away with something wrong and unfair. Some think that forgiving is the same as saying the violation, whatever it was, was okay. However, this could not be further from the truth.

An act of forgiveness is, in fact, an act of great strength.

We think that if we hang on to upsetting experiences through our thoughts and words, then we are giving a clear message to the other person that we are stronger and better than they are and we will not let them forget it!

But ultimately, who are we hurting by carrying around past suffering with us?

Could it be that we're hurting ourselves? Could it be that the other person has moved on and that we are the ones who are powerless, allowing the actions of another to control our lives and hold us back? Could <u>we</u> be "drinking poison" while expecting the other person to "die"?

If you think the answer might be "yes," consider these three reasons why it makes perfect sense that only strong individuals are able to forgive:

1.   IT'S A VIBRATION

Every thought, word, action, and feeling has a vibration. When you approach the concept of forgiveness from the perspective of the energy or vibration it produces and requires, it takes on an entirely new meaning.

You will see that the qualities associated with forgiveness - love, peace, happiness - are fast, high, empowering vibrational energies.

On the contrary, the qualities associated with not forgiving—resentment, anger, hatred—are slow, low, disempowering energies. When you are unforgiving, you throw that negative vibrational energy out into the Universe for yourself—not them—you!

Forgiveness is not about the other person. Forgiveness is about taking back the power that you have relinquished to the offender.

It is a display of courage and inner strength. It shows that you have so much love for yourself that you will not allow your happiness to be stolen from you.

Exhibiting a peaceful nature shows that you are too strong to be stained by others' petty words and behaviors. This shows that you are above the insults and brutality of the other person.

Their actions are a reflection of their issues and have nothing to do with you and who you are.

2.   IT'S A MATTER OF FREEDOM

After much of his life had been unfairly spent behind bars,

Nelson Mandela said,
"As I walked out the door toward the gate
that would lead to my freedom,
I knew if I didn't leave my bitterness and
hatred behind, I'd still be in prison."

So, you must ask yourself, "Am I living in an invisible prison because I am unable to forgive?"

Refusing to forgive is a prison of the heart and mind. People who have hurt you are the cell walls, and your thoughts about them are the steel bars keeping you inside. Without forgiveness, moving forward is impossible; the future is limited, and you become stagnant. By holding on to your pain, you turn the controls of your emotional life over to someone else. There is no freedom in that. Hanging on to suffering only hurts you more. Forgiveness and letting go put you in a place of power and freedom. The person who benefits is you.

3.   IT'S ABOUT BEING HUMAN

Everyone has been both the giver and recipient of meanness, hostility, and insensitivity. That includes you and me. It takes a certain degree of awareness and elevation in consciousness to recognize that each soul who crosses your path is doing the best they can at their level of understanding. The person that has hurt you is a human being too.

We all make mistakes. No one is immune. And because of our humanness, internalizing the slow, debilitating energies of resentment and anger cause us harm. It blocks our prosperity, our goodness, our happiness, and above all, our peace.

Forgiveness has nothing to do with the other person and does not condone their behavior in any way. I'm not suggesting that you have a love fest with the person. They do not need to be involved in you forgiving them. They don't even need to be on the planet at this point. But what I am suggesting is that you

quietly contemplate what your life would be like without their negative influence.

It's important to do so. Possibly, the person that you need to forgive is you.

Forgiveness is a gift that you give to yourself.

The highest form of self-love is self-forgiveness. The act of forgiving someone is, in essence, your refusal to let anger and hatred prevent you from moving forward. You are taking a stand against allowing the actions of others to alter the course of your life or who you are.

Being able to forgive is admirable and shows great courage. Those who cannot forgive are letting their ego get in the way. They do not want to forgive, which only serves to weaken them in all aspects of their life.

Being strong enough to free one's self from the prison of not forgiving is a choice.

It is a chance to be reborn, to fill your mind with peace, to heal, and move on. And within that energy lies unlimited strength.

LET'S TAKE ACTION! WORKSHEET:

Let's Talk About Forgiveness

1) Forgiveness is a gift that you give to yourself. Who can you forgive in order to let YOURSELF be free? Ask yourself, "Am I living in an invisible prison because I am unable to forgive?". How so?

2) Can you think of a time when you have wanted forgiveness from someone else? How did it feel when you did or did not receive their forgiveness?

3) Self-love is self-forgiveness - can you forgive yourself for something you've been holding onto?

Life Script #21

The Purpose of Hurt

The Purpose of *Hurt*

—— . . . ——

Everyone thinks of having their feelings hurt as a negative experience. How could it not be, right? But can it actually serve us in some way?

Well, the truth is that "hurt" is a powerful and positive experience once we understand its real purpose.

Just because the experience is negative doesn't mean that the message it's giving is, as well. We are being guided at all times to access our power.

> *Believe it or not, our negative feelings are always directing us to acknowledge an inner strength and to become empowered.*

Consider these three profound messages hiding behind the emotional pain we endure:

1. TRUE CALLING

When you go through something that makes you feel fearful, uneasy, or sad, it means that you are not a vibrational match to it. That's a good thing! It says that it is not what you want for yourself in your life. It is the opposite of your truth. It contrasts with your vibration. There is meaning in the contrast. It brings greater clarity and points you in another direction.

Many people are suffering in jobs that drain the joy from their lives. This is a huge red flag! They are participating in an activity that opposes their joy. Or maybe you're the type of person who has faced much pain and suffering throughout your life. Could this mean that you have a natural ability to be a healer to others?

How about someone who is fearful of meeting people? The negative emotion of fear is telling them that they don't want to meet anyone new because they don't want to feel the fear. But it could be that they would benefit by embodying the opposite, positive energy, which is that of being a great communicator.

The contradictory vibration is guiding you to what may end up being your true calling in life.

You have to ask yourself, "Is this something that resonates with me and makes me happy? Do I feel in vibrational alignment with this situation?"

Of course, if the feeling is uncomfortable and makes you unhappy, then no, you are not in vibrational alignment. This means that the opposite, comfortable situation is what does align with you vibrationally, and merits a closer look. It may be your ultimate talent, gift, and life's calling. This is how weakness becomes strength.

First, determine how you feel while doing something. You will know when a person or event is a good match by the good, easy feeling it or they inspire in you.

2. RISE ABOVE

Hurt comes in many forms. Most commonly, it triggers our sense of being devalued.

Emotional hurt activates any underlying feelings of low self-esteem that we're holding onto.

Now, if those feelings weren't triggered or activated, we would never be able to acknowledge, address, and rise above them. Unfortunately, the intensity of this type of wake-up call can be brutal.

It happens in an uncomfortable way to motivate us into action, to strengthen and develop us.

Experiencing this kind of hurt is meant to empower. If we don't view it and understand it as such, then

we will continue to be devalued by others until we get the message.

It might take many years and many relationships with family, friends, coworkers, and partners before we realize that we are valuable.

Again, what is being brought to our attention by not feeling good (because it is the opposite of our truth) is that somewhere inside of us, we don't believe we are good enough. This belief is not who we are and is showing up so that you can squarely address it and let it go.

We're being shown where we are not in alignment with what is true.

Every time we feel hurt is a grand opportunity to rise above the negative conditioning and live according to our authentic nature, which is in direct connection to our inner strength.

3. RESPONSIBILITY

No one wants to hear that they aren't taking responsibility for their life. However, when we feel hurt then assign blame to others for our hurt feelings, this is exactly what we're doing.

What I mean is that by placing blame on another person or situation, we are, in essence, giving them all the power. When we say, "They did this to me!" or "They let this happen!" or "It's because of this or that," what we are doing is claiming our lack of power over the situation. This way, we don't have to assume responsibility for the messes in our lives.

The point is, when we feel the need to blame someone or something, we are not getting the message as to why the situation occurred in the first place. The reason is not simply "because that person is a jerk." That person may well be a jerk, but the deeper meaning of the encounter was for you to recognize your power, the power to create your life the way you want it to be. No person or situation has that ability over you unless you give it to them.

Taking responsibility is about finding that powerful part of yourself and applying it, which can only benefit your existence. So even though having negative emotions wrapped around certain moments and chapters in life can be difficult, those times hold a very important purpose for each one of us.

When we're in the moment,
this truth may be impossible to see.

However, when the smoke has cleared and we're no longer enveloped in our suffering, hopefully we can take a minute and recognize that

we've been given an extraordinary opportunity
to know ourselves on a more profound level and
to more fully embody who we truly are.

This knowledge allows us to make worthwhile use of those painful times. Let's not waste it.

LET'S TAKE ACTION! WORKSHEET:

The Purpose of Hurt

1) Which of the three profound messages hiding behind the emotional pain we endure resonated most with you and why?

_____

_____

_____

_____

_____

_____

_____

2) Think of a specific past emotional pain. Can you reframe it below to have had a greater purpose?

_____

_____

_____

_____

_____

_____

_____

_____

Life Script #22

Why Most People Are
Deathly Afraid of
Public Speaking
and What They Can
Do About It

Why Most People Are Deathly Afraid of
Public Speaking
and What They Can Do About It

— • • • —

It has been repeated by many and joked about by the likes of Jerry Seinfeld that most people are more afraid of public speaking than death itself. And even though this statement may be quite amusing, it lacks scientific truth. However, research has shown that public speaking is one of the most common social phobias.

For instance, when you receive an amazing opportunity to give a talk on a particular subject in your field of expertise, or a live interview on the radio or TV, do you immediately jump to a place inside yourself of sheer panic? Does your heart race? Breathing stop? Mind go totally blank? Well, if the mere thought of having to put yourself out there like that leaves you terrified, then consider doing these three things to alleviate the stress of it all, and instead, feel confident and prepared for such a situation:

1. MAKE FRIENDS WITH YOUR INNER CAVEWOMAN OR CAVEMAN

You may not be aware of this, but each one of us has a cavewoman or caveman living inside our bodies. She or he is one of the many parts of the self. When our inner caveperson feels "singled-out,"

primitive instincts kick in,

telling us that we are no longer part of a group, and therefore, survival is slim to none. After all, how are you going to fight off a saber-toothed tiger all by yourself? It can make us feel threatened in a life or death kind of way.

But the cavewoman or caveman simply lacks understanding.

*The reactionary piece of ourselves
Thinks it is protecting us from harm.*

So when he or she starts acting out, trying to get your attention by alerting you to something it sees as a danger, don't ignore it. The challenge of being able to control our nerves only gets harder when we seek to "kill off" that scared side of us, trying to force the mind to pay it no attention.

What happens next is the caveperson's voice and influence become louder and stronger as it fears even more for your/its life! At that point, panic sets in, indicating that he or she has gained way too much power and has created a major imbalance of who's in charge.

To regain control and balance of our nerves, we have to do the opposite. We have to see that primitive part of the self for what it is—just another hat each of us wears on a daily basis.

Embrace this piece of yourself; have compassion for that which resides within and doesn't understand.

*When you experience fear,
recognize where it is coming from,*

i.e., this frightened cavewoman or caveman inside that is merely wanting to protect you. So take care of them, sit them down in the corner for now, make them a nice hot cup of tea, give them reassurance, a big hug, and put them down for a nice, long nap. Then go and put on a different hat of yours.

Picture your cavewoman or caveman as a cute little character that just needs your love and understanding. Each time you do, he or she will become less and less vocal and less in charge, because you both will gradually be able to relate to one another and realize that your relationship is based purely in self-love.

2. GET OUT YOUR SMARTPHONE

Find a quiet place where you won't be interrupted, even if it's your car or the bathroom, and interview yourself. Take out your phone and record yourself speaking. Answer questions about your work and your life. Explain the new project you've been working on or the new information you have to share with the world. Play it back.

As you hear your voice, recognize ways to tweak the words you use to make them sound more interesting. Maybe you notice that you're talking too fast or aren't enunciating. This exercise will not only bring much more self-confidence but will allow you to form patented answers to questions that can flow right off your tongue when the real situation arises.

Once you're comfortable with this process, take small steps into exposure. Ask a friend, then two, then more to sit and listen to you respond to their questions or be the audience to your presentation. Standing in front of a small group and getting their feedback will greatly shore up your courage!

3. SEE IT BEFORE YOU DO IT

There is so much validity to visualizing an experience before it happens. Athletes the world over will tell you that it is essential to their performance. When you get up to speak in front of a group of people, it is a performance. You are just like an actor, musician, or athlete.

They all have to rehearse their material. They visualize themselves doing it over and over again, thinking of ways to improve and enhance their execution of their role. They not only practice for real, they practice in their mind's eye. They notice all of the senses involved at that moment and anchor them into reality.

They create the memory of having already reached their goal.

It's like training a muscle. If you don't use it, then it doesn't get stronger. So build that weak muscle and see yourself accomplishing the feat!

Being the center of attention can feel extremely unnatural to many people. Being put on the spot to display one's knowledge or skill can also feel terribly uncomfortable and scary. The key to overcoming these emotions is to be prepared and recognize that our fears stem not from a lack of self-worth, but quite the opposite. Our fears are born out of a deep sense of love for the self that wants nothing more than to protect us and keep us safe. Be grateful for it and show compassion for its intent.

LET'S TAKE ACTION! WORKSHEET:

Public Speaking

1) On a scale of 1 - 10, where would you rate your fear of public speaking and why?

_____

_____

_____

2) The next time you have a public speaking engagement, what are you going to tell yourself?

_____

_____

_____

_____

_____

_____

_____

_____

"To give and not expect return,
that is what lies at the heart of love"

-Oscar Wilde

The *Art* of Giving and Receiving

Life
Script
#23

The Golden Rule of
Energy

The Golden Rule of *Energy*

· · ·

"Do unto others as you would have them do unto you." Sound familiar? Those are powerful words to live by. But when placed in the context of giving and receiving energy, the Golden Rule takes on profound significance. This invisible exchange of energy creates a bond between the Golden Rule and the Law of Cause and Effect. Therefore, not only is it important to be aware that treating others the way we would like to be treated is morally the right thing to do, but it is just as important to understand that for every one of our actions, there is an equal and opposite reaction that we draw toward ourselves. In other words, what goes around comes around.

Here are three ways we sometimes make the mistake of ignoring the Golden Rule and how the Law of Cause and Effect makes us pay for it every single time:

1. BESMIRCHING A REPUTATION

Wishing another person ill will, spreading gossip and rumors, and judging or criticizing another's success, either personally or professionally, invites that same behavior from others into your own life. It's the boomerang effect.

Whenever you're tempted to speak out against another person's life choices, whether most people would agree with you or not, just stop and think, "Is this what I want for myself? Do I want other people saying these things about me?"

You should never do something to others that you do not want to experience yourself.

When you hear people talking in an unflattering or hateful way about someone else, and you join in, how does it make you feel? Superior? Important?

Try keeping these words of wisdom in the back of your mind,

*"It's nice to be important,
but it's more important to be nice."*

Stand up for others. You would want them to stand up for you. If you consistently follow the Golden Rule, the Law of Cause and Effect will consistently have your back.

2. LEAVING GOOD DEEDS UNDONE

Making others feel special and valued is necessary. Don't we all like to feel that way? This is not just about showing respect toward another person, although that of course is essential.
No, this is about going out of your way and making the effort to do a good deed that you know you didn't have to do, but wanted to do because you knew it would make someone else feel good. It doesn't matter if it's in regard to your business interactions, your loved ones, or for a complete stranger.

For instance, maybe there is a charity that you've heard needs volunteers and donations. You know you don't have to help out. You also know you won't directly be receiving any compensation for it. But you decide to make a contribution of time or money simply because it will benefit another soul, put a smile on their face, and hopefully make their life a little easier.

Taking action and having the awareness that you could be the one in need of assistance given a different set of circumstances, and that if you were in that position, you would appreciate being treated with the same compassion, will bring abundance to you through other sources.

Making others feel good makes you feel good too.

Doing nice things for people raises your vibration and puts you in alignment to receive positive situations in your life. Good feelings are simply magnets for experiences that cause you to feel more good feelings. You serve yourself by serving others. In doing what's right for others, you cause the right things to be done for you.

3. BEING DISCOURAGING

There is a time and place for practicality. However, I firmly believe that

when you discourage someone from following their dreams, you block or delay the happiness, abundance, and prosperity

that would otherwise be headed in your direction. Why? Because you are interfering with another individual's life path, dissuading them from doing what they love, and possibly keeping them from experiencing the joy of living their purpose on this earth

Elevate others and you elevate yourself.

Who are we to say that another person's dreams and passions are wrong? Most visionaries that have changed the course of humanity in the fields of technology, medicine, art, and many other professions were discouraged and considered foolish or completely off their rockers. They didn't listen to their opposition and became great men and women of history.

Just think where we would be without all of the inventions and breakthroughs that have propelled us through the ages. Encouraging a person to pursue their ideas, aspirations, and talents not only has an extremely powerful and positive effect on their own life but yours as well. Building people up changes lives. Tearing them down does too. On which side would you rather be?

Each day, we should spend time contemplating which of our actions do or do not add value to the human experience. The only way to assess this is to feel. We've been created with a tangible mechanism called emotion. This is our natural GPS. It tells us when we are aligned with our highest good and, in essence, are causing an effect that supports the highest good of all.

Our happiness comes when we follow this built-in guidance system. Our unhappiness comes when we veer off course. Listen to your GPS where others are concerned, and act accordingly. You will most certainly be rewarded. It's a rule and a law!

LET'S TAKE ACTION! WORKSHEET:

What Goes Around Comes Around...

We just discovered the three ways we sometimes make the mistake of ignoring the Golden Rule and how the Law of Cause and Effect makes us pay for it every single time. Let's examine each of them:

1) Recall a time when you may have wished another person ill will, spread gossip and rumors, judged or criticized another's success, either personally or professionally:

_____

_____

_____

The next time you catch yourself doing this, what will you remind yourself?

_____

_____

_____

2) What can you do today (without expecting anything in return) to make someone feel special and valued?

_____

_____

_____

3) Can you remember a time when you may have discouraged someone from following their dreams? Next time, what will you do instead?

_____

_____

_____

Life Script #24

The Key to Receiving
the Life of Your
Dreams

The Key to Receiving the Life of Your *Dreams*

——— • • • ———

When it comes to everyday living, do you feel like you have to control all the "whos," "hows," "whats," "whens," "wheres," and "whys," or else life will be even more difficult? When circumstances don't go exactly the way you planned, do you feel like they've gone wrong? If this sounds familiar, why not be kinder to yourself and open up to the possibility that life could be a lot easier if you'd only let it?

Just assume for a moment that all of your limited "whens," "hows," etc. are totally incorrect. Stop and consider that

you may be trying to force your life into something it isn't meant to be.

What if, instead, you are keeping your life from going smoothly and being more enjoyable?

Take a look at the ways in which you approach your life every day. Maybe all you need is a change of perspective to allow your life to work for you, not against you:

1. FORCING OR ALLOWING

Instead of searching for answers, pushing to make things happen, and constantly looking to the future for happiness and satisfaction, try letting life unfold more naturally.

*When we're always searching,
we're living in a position of lack.
Our focus is on what we don't have,
what's missing.*

If we relax and become open to guidance from unexpected places, information is shown to us in ways we never thought possible. People and situations are brought into our lives to take us down a perfectly orchestrated path we hadn't even considered.

We may not know the people yet, or be aware of the events that are going on behind the scenes, but the answers will come "when" and "how" it is in our best interests. The answers will find us.

Trying to force events to happen in your life will only delay the abundance and prosperity that is supposed to flow in your direction. When you feel like you're "spinning your wheels" and getting nowhere, even though you're working yourself into a frenzy, it's because you are going nowhere! What you are doing is resisting.

A natural process is trying to take place, and you are pushing for an unnatural process to occur instead. Feeling out of balance like that will never align you with what you need and want in your life. Stress, frustration, anger, and depression are all signs that you are fighting against life.

These feelings are strong messages that you are on the wrong track.

The present is where all things exist, and all things have a particular vibration. That which is happy and fulfilling vibrates on a high, positive level. That which is upsetting and draining vibrates on a low, negative level. So in order to draw to us the satisfaction and joy we crave,

we cannot be stressed out today in an attempt to create something wonderful tomorrow. The vibrations don't match. We will never get there.

What we want is already out there somewhere. We just have to align ourselves with our desire by being centered on the same positive vibrational level. Choose to be happy now, not sometime in the future.

2. FEARING OR TRUSTING

When unforeseen circumstances pop up in your life, do you automatically assume the worst? Do you go straight to the negative?

The best advice is to not even go there!

As soon as you slide into a low, fear-based vibration, you not only attract more circumstances that will make you fearful because they are vibrating at the same low level, you also build a wall that blocks any solution from presenting itself.

All situations arise for a reason. Trust that there is a plan for your life that's going to play out whether you're on board with it or not. You can create delays by resisting and being fearful, or you can create an open door for the plan to proceed through with ease. It's your choice. You have the power to make things hard on yourself.

The less you react and simply move on, the better.

Do your best to avoid giving negative situations any energy,

and you will avoid making them worse. Trust in the process that all things naturally work themselves out.

3. FIXING OR HELPING

When you feel the need to "help" someone live a better life, are you acting out of love and compassion for that human being, or are you trying to "fix" them? It may seem like a fine line, but when you think you can actually "fix" someone's life for them, what you're doing is making judgments about them.

In your opinion, and maybe in several people's opinions, this person is wrong in the way they choose to think and act. But who are you or anyone else to decide what particular path they are on? Who are we to say what lessons they are here to learn? Each person is only responsible for navigating their particular path. There is no way to know what we or any other human being is meant to experience in this lifetime.

Maybe someone is always "pushing your buttons" with their negativity, trying to gain inappropriate attention. What you have to do is emotionally detach from their

"Trauma drama".

Even if you live with them, tell them you're sorry they're having a bad day, then walk away.

And don't believe that going into another room and thinking about it or being angry and giving them the silent treatment is detaching from it, because it isn't.

You are still fueling the situation because you are still giving it energy.

If you're set on helping, pull your energy back by giving them the freedom and space

to express whatever it is they feel they need to express, then let it go. As soon as you do, you will almost immediately notice a shift in them. You'll be amazed at how they improve their attitude and the direction of their life all on their own.

All of us on this planet are guided, and hopefully, at some point become compelled to live the life of our dreams. It happens when we relinquish control of the process. Only then can we hold our hands out to the Universe and receive, receive, receive.

LET'S TAKE ACTION! WORKSHEET:

Time to change your perspective...

What changes of perspective can you make to allow your life to work for you, not against you? What do you think you can specifically change in your life to receive the life of your dreams?

Life Script #25

When Giving is Not a Good Thing

When *Giving* is Not a Good Thing

— • • • —

There is, indeed, an art to giving and receiving. And never is that more abundantly clear when gift-giving.

At festive or celebratory times of year, most people are racking their brains trying to figure out what presents to buy for each other. The act of giving and receiving should be pretty easy for us to handle, though, right? So why does it get so frustrating and complicated?

We give with strings attached, sometimes too little, other times too much. Giving should enhance our lives and bring us joy, not create more stress and consternation.

I believe that giving and receiving joy, whatever form that takes, is one of the main reasons we are on this planet together. However, at times I think we lose sight of our best intentions.

So to avoid turning the act of giving into a negative experience for the giver, the receiver, or both, here is some food for thought when going shopping for gifts for the people in your life:

1. GIVING TOO MUCH OR TOO LITTLE

Any healthy relationship has an equal amount of give and take. So, contrary to the saying, "It's better to give than to receive," you must be both a giver and receiver for abundance to flow because giving and receiving stimulate one another. Consequently, an uneven exchange, an imbalance, stops the flow.

Some people are always giving, but not receiving. That type of scenario can eventually leave the giver feeling utterly depleted and resentful. Giving too much may result in the giver playing the martyr. In turn, those who give so that they will get something back or give out of guilt are neither giving nor receiving. It becomes a contest determining who gives or gets more stuff. Then that stuff becomes the measure of one's self-worth. That's not a healthy position to take.

2. GIVING WITHOUT VALUE

When something is given without value, it is not worth giving or receiving. Whether a gift has value has to do with the intention behind it.

You only truly give when the intention is love.

When we give (and it doesn't matter if the gift costs money or not), we need to ask ourselves if we are giving out of obligation and/or sheer convenience. How much did you sincerely try?

You may not realize it, but the energy of your half-hearted intention is carried along with your "gift" to the recipient. Don't you think they can feel that you didn't show care? It is important to always be thankful for what we are given, but have you ever considered that gifts given without "value" can actually hurt the other person?

3. GIVING WHAT YOU WANT

From an energetic point of view, when you give to others with love based on **their** needs and wishes, the Universe mirrors that intention and brings you that which best aligns with your needs and wishes.

However, sometimes we get self-absorbed and assume everybody wants what we want. How could they not, right?

Even though you may mean well, it's important to put yourself in their shoes for a moment. When a gift shows little or no consideration for the other person's personality or interests but instead fits your own, then it just looks like it's all about you, not them. Be honest and say to yourself, "Would they enjoy this gift? It doesn't matter if I would enjoy receiving it or not; it isn't about me."

Everyone always says, "It's the thought that counts!" My question is, "What thoughts are we thinking?"

So next time your gift giving, keep this in mind: focus on the joy, then maintain that giving nature and be of service to one another throughout the entire year.

LET'S TAKE ACTION! WORKSHEET:

The Art of Giving - Pop Quiz!

Fill in the below according to what you just read. If you get stumped, don't worry - just re-visit the previous pages for the answers:

1) Any healthy relationship has an equal amount of .... and ....

2) Everyone always says, "It's the thought that counts!" The question is, ...

3) What are the 3 things to keep in mind to avoid turning the act of giving into a negative experience for the giver, the receiver, or both?

1. ....

2. ....

3. ....

4) Circle the correct answer:

You only truly give when the intention is:

Happiness   Selfish   Love   Hate

Keep it up: Next time you're out shopping for gifts, be sure to revisit this chapter!

Life Script #26

How Random Acts of *Kindness* Change Reality

How Random Acts of *Kindness* Change Reality

———— . . . ————

Have you ever stopped to think about what random acts of kindness do? I mean, sure, they make you feel pretty good about yourself and make somebody else feel pretty good, too.

But have you ever considered their impact on an energetic level? It might surprise you to learn that the small gesture you made toward someone this morning had a far-reaching, powerful, lasting effect on the planet.

How, you say? Well, here are three big ways you just changed the world:

1. PERCEPTION OF LIFE

When you participate in a random act of kindness, what you are doing, in essence, is giving and receiving love,

unconditional love,

no strings attached,

no feeling of obligation.

When you are giving, you acknowledge the goodness in your life and the spiritual presence that is always at work encouraging you to continue to connect with others, to give love and compassion without the expectation of reward or recognition. Spending time looking for ways to express unconditional love toward other human beings, and imagining how creating that connection will make you and them feel, will leave no room for depression in your life.

When we do something on behalf of another, we can think of ourselves as being half of it. That means we do not sacrifice or hurt ourselves to help another. It means we become part of the help and receive help in the process.

An elevation takes place in your vibration and spirit when you think of how you contributed to another person's well-being.

The focus is taken off of you and any challenges you may be having and is placed on what you can do on behalf of another dear soul. As you act on those thoughts with the purest of intentions, life becomes a new, hopeful experience to joyfully embrace.

Giving to others is never about doing without. It is about making greater room within to receive. You may not have much to give at this time in your life, but what makes the act of giving so special is showing that you do the best you can with what you have. Maybe it's just a smile or opening the door for someone. A quality life does not depend on how much you have. It depends on how much you have given of your heart.

2. UNIVERSAL SHIFT

Random acts of kindness are feedback loops of positive energy creation. Helping others not only raises your vibration but also the vibrations of those you help and that of the entire human collective. Creating something unexpected and wonderful in someone else's life, no matter how small, sets into motion a dramatic shift in a positive direction that can profoundly change lives.

You can never really know how deep of an impact you've made in someone's life. What you consider a little bit of kindness may turn a person's life completely around and give them hope for the future. The Universe responds to these shifts by bringing more and more abundance to you, them, and everyone on the planet. Changing another's reality through your actions has a ripple effect, which changes the world . . .

3. HUMANITY'S EVOLUTION

Performing random acts of kindness makes you an example of what is possible.

*You become an inspiration,
opening the awareness of others to their own potential.*

Most of us want our lives to inspire love in others. So, for instance, when our children witness us doing good in the world, they are taught gratitude, compassion, love, and unity. Each generation learns this way.

Happiness is a choice, but you have to be open to it and take action to help spread it around. The world is evolving in such a way that it requires each of us to take responsibility toward creating and nurturing positive energy any way we can. We are transforming the old methods or expressions into newer, lighter, more loving ways of being and living. The most important thing we can do is send our love out into the world, no matter what form it takes.

A simple random act of kindness could very easily be life-giving to both the giver and receiver. When one is coming from a place of generosity, of giving and kindness that is pure without any expectation of reward in return, what is occurring is the manifestation of a deeper reality,

a deeper understanding that you are not so alone,

that you are united and connected to more than you may have ever realized.

LET'S TAKE ACTION! WORKSHEET:

Random Acts of Kindness Challenge!

See if you can come up with 10 random acts of kindness ideas below! (If you get stumped, ask a friend or person around you for some ideas)

1. _____

2. _____

3. _____

4. _____

5. _____

6. _____

7. _____

8. _____

9. _____

10. _____

Next, pick 3 of your above ideas that would not be too complicated to complete. Commit to doing one each day for the next 3 days. Schedule it below so you stick to it!

Act of Kindess: When I will do it:

1. _____   Day & Time: _____

2. _____   Day & Time: _____

3. _____   Day & Time: _____

Keep it up: Can you choose 4 more random acts of kindness and schedule them in so that you can do a daily act of kindness every day this week?

Now share the challenge with your friends and encourage them to try it too.

LET'S TAKE ACTION! WORKSHEET:

Reflection...

Below, write about the random acts of kindness you performed. How did they make you feel? What was the receiver's reaction? Was there one that particularly stood out to you? Why?

"All you need is love"

-The Beatles

CHAPTER 6

How To
Love

Life Script #27

Do You Love Yourself?

Do You *Love* Yourself?

The question "Do you love yourself?" is, in fact, not a simple question at all. And that goes for possibly the majority of people on the planet. For many, it can be a terribly painful question.

But we must all realize that the most important thing we can do is shower <u>ourselves</u> with love and attention. Don't expect or wait for someone else to do it. Instead, consider these three ways to be able to love yourself:

1. REALIZE YOU ARE WHOLE

If we're looking for someone or something outside ourselves to complete us, we will inevitably be disappointed.

Wholeness can only be experienced within the self. If parts of you feel incomplete, send love to those aspects and think about where the sense of incompleteness is coming from. Reflect upon actions you could take and attitudes you could change to feel whole within.

You are whole and complete right now at this very moment.

So keep in mind that when you want to know what the future holds, sometimes you miss completely the present moment you are supposed to be having and experiencing.

2. BEEP. BEEP. BEEP. BACK IT UP!

We have to allow others the right not to accept our love. Sometimes we expend a lot of energy that doesn't seem to be returned in kind. We may be trying to reach a certain person to get his or her attention, gratitude, or love only to be ignored or even rejected completely.

When this happens, take a step back and examine

why we continue to give our best to those who are neither ready nor willing to accept it.

Love and connectedness can come to us only when the other person desires the same thing and is open—not closed—to our energy.

If we experience repeated blockages in a relationship, we first need to

withdraw our energy so that it can breathe and we can heal.

Then we need to reconnect to our inner strength and reaffirm our value, our goodness, and our right to have genuinely loving relationships.

Are your relationships generally fulfilling and energizing or frustrating and draining?

Is there anyone in your life who is not accepting the energy you are sending? If so, ask yourself why you continue to put out the energy and engage in an uneven exchange?

Allow the person the right to not receive your energy, and reflect upon where you could better direct your efforts. Learn the secret of how much to give and receive in your relationships.

3. TREAT YOURSELF

Treat yourself to a wonderful life!

Treat yourself with kindness and compassion.

You can also treat yourself with material items. Is there a pretty outfit or piece of jewelry you've had your eye on? Buy it for yourself! Would you love some fragrant flowers to make you happy? Send them to yourself!

Last year, I had to pick out a birthday card for myself on behalf of my father who no longer drives because he wanted to make sure I received a card from him. Surprisingly enough, that was one of the most fun experiences of my life. I could be anything I wanted. And I'll tell you right now, according to that card, I am the most fabulous person I have ever met. Who knew?

We are on the earth to take care of ourselves first. Only then will we be able to truly care about another's well-being. Do you treat other people, even strangers, better than you treat yourself? We can be our own best friend or worst enemy. Which do you choose?

Look in the mirror and say, "I love you." Can you do it? Keep saying it over and over again. You may become very emotional and say it through your tears. This is healing. You are all you need.

You are truly perfect exactly as you are and can have, be, and do whatever you choose for yourself.

Remember that the future is not ours to see, but it is ours to create. As you live in the present moment to the best of your abilities, you create the future you were meant to have. Know that there is a magnificent plan for your life. By loving yourself, you give this unique plan permission to unfold.

LET'S TAKE ACTION! WORKSHEET:

Loving Yourself

On a scale of 1 - 10, how much would you say you truly love yourself? (This answer can change greatly, even throughout the day!)

Do you treat other people, even strangers, better than you treat yourself?

We can be our own best friend or worst enemy. Which do you choose?

What are some actions you could take and attitudes you could change to feel whole within?

Are your relationships generally fulfilling and energizing or frustrating and draining? Is there anyone in your life who is not accepting the energy you are sending? If so, ask yourself why you continue to put out the energy and engage in an uneven exchange?

What can you do today to treat YOURSELF and show yourself some love?

Life Script #28

What Would *Love* Do?

What Would 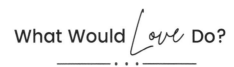 Do?

———— • • • ————

When we search for love in all its forms, we may be surprised where we find it. Much of the time, love does not appear to us as what we have been conditioned to recognize. Love does not always make everyone comfortable. Love does not always please. Love is not always cheery and positive. Being loving does not mean throwing away our personal boundaries.

Consider these three scenarios that are expressions of love in disguise:

1. LOVE SAYS "NO"

There are times when "no" is an expression of love.

Being honest with yourself and others is an action that comes from a place of love.

It may require others to learn the lesson of discomfort. Sometimes love, at the moment, is about nurturing oneself and not someone else.

Love is being honest with requests for help. If you want to help a friend, then by all means do so. If your heart, however, feels as though it's being made to do something that doesn't truly resonate, then say "no".

We naturally experience burnout when we compassionately and lovingly attempt to assist others, but that's because we are not first treating ourselves with at least that same love and compassion. The result is depletion, a draining of our energy when instead, our energy should always be replenished. How can we help others if we have nothing left to give?

2. LOVE DOES NOT TOLERATE ABUSE

Love does not tolerate abuse in any form: physical or emotional. Abuse can take the shape of intimidation, control, or neglect. It isn't loving to allow yourself to be dishonored, nor is it loving to allow abusers to continue dishonoring you or themselves through their behavior. If a close relationship does not honor you, celebrate you, or nurture you, then love is showing you that it is time for it to end.

Love may require tremendous courage and feel very lonely.

Be your own loving parent, guide, and best friend. And know that insisting upon safe, loving connections in your inner circle is the only way love wants you to live.

3. LOVE HAS NOT-SO-PROUD MOMENTS

You were trying. You were seeking love. Love allows self-acceptance of our negative emotions. Love is brewing beneath those angry outbursts wherein we demand better treatment for ourselves.

Love can boil and bubble up to the surface to let you know in no uncertain terms that it has better for you. Love is all there is. Therefore, sadness, anger, and fear can possibly be the highest expression of love available to you in that moment.

It shows us where we are bound by the chains of disharmony and limiting beliefs, so we can break free of them. Love may not express itself in a happy, positive fashion. It may express itself by making us uncomfortable and unhappy so that we see there must be a better way.

Love is strength. It is where we hold our power. Love may demand our bravery. It may be the wrecking ball that crashes through the walls in our lives, revealing where healing is needed. So, just allow love to do what it must in your life because the results will always give you wings to fly.

LET'S TAKE ACTION! WORKSHEET:

W.W.L.D?

(What Would Love Do?)

Can you think of some real-life scenario examples that are expressions of love in disguise?

Life
Script #29

What is Your *Intention*?

What is Your  ?

—— . . . ——

Success and failure are proportionate to intention.

If your intention is love, you will be successful in any situation or undertaking, no matter what it is.

This is because there is an invisible force, a vibration that carries your intention to its audience.

When you do something, whether it's writing a book, spearheading a project at work, going on a diet, or helping your children with their homework, your actions and words will not be well-received if you hold the feeling that you are doing it because you have to.

The outcome of everything you say and do depends on your approach. Are you approaching the task from a place of love, or are you coming from a place of fear, obligation, or resentment?

Stop for a moment. Say to yourself,

"I am love."

A change in your disposition is inevitable. You will have aligned your vibration with the vibration of love, the highest level there is. Those around you will suddenly feel this change of atmosphere and react and respond accordingly. They will inadvertently align with you. It's the same feeling you have when someone walks into a room. Do you automatically feel good or bad being around that person?

When you are faced with something that you don't want to do but feel you have to do, take a step back and find a way to see it from the perspective of your heart, not your head. Changing the way that you see a challenging situation will shift your experience of it.

Answer the following questions to turn life obligations into fulfilling experiences:

1. ARE YOU HELPING ANOTHER?

Realize the good that will come from your assistance, even if it's just for one person in need. You will make a lasting imprint with your words and actions. So understand that whatever it is you are doing,

*it's not about you.
It's about being of service to someone
who needs you and will benefit from your help.*

2. WHAT ARE YOU ATTRACTING?

When you radiate love, you are attracting love back to you. When you radiate anger and resentment, you are attracting that, too.

You can feel the energy of people you've been in contact with, can't you? Even if it's just from a phone call, it's palpable. It's hard to not take on that other person's persona, good or bad. Do you want to attract resistance and bad attitudes from others in regards to you and your endeavors? Then don't have a bad attitude, because you will cause yourself to fail in that endeavor —every time.

3. WHAT IF YOU LIVE AS AN EXAMPLE?

All of us need someone to inspire and encourage us, adults and children alike. Children, in particular, learn what they live. So if you are impatient and easily agitated with your child, don't be surprised when he or she becomes impatient and easily agitated with you.

Demonstrate for your coworkers how your relationships can be. Live in possibility. They, too, need to be motivated and elevated to a new level so they can feel good about what they do.

Positive energy is contagious.
So is negative energy.

Negative energy will kill a business, or a marriage, or anything it infects. "Garbage in, garbage out," as they say. Set a positive example by coming from a place of love, and your energy will lift those around you. The result will be great success!

Align your feelings and endeavors with the highest vibration in the Universe—love—and success will always be yours.

 **LET'S TAKE ACTION! WORKSHEET:**

Making obligations fulfilling!

Next time you are faced with something that you don't want to do but feel you have to do, take a step back and find a way to see it from the perspective of your heart, not your head. Changing the way that you see a challenging situation will shift your experience of it.

Answer these questions to change your intention and lead with love:

1) Am I Helping Another?

2) What Am I Attracting?

3) What If I Live as an Example?

Life Script #30

The One Reason We Are All On The Planet

The One Reason We Are All On The Planet

The one and only reason we are on the planet is this:

To learn to love.

We are here to learn to love ourselves, each other, the planet itself, and all living beings. Every day we are put in situations that give us the opportunity to do just that.

We are constantly presented with experiences where we need to exhibit compassion. This opening may show up in the form of an abused dog that a person is called to rescue, or the creation of a new campaign to provide clean water to areas of Africa because there is a need.

The answer to why something happened the way it did is always that you or the person involved is still learning to love.

It encompasses every challenge we face as the human race. So whenever we see something that tugs at our hearts, we must recognize the moment as offering us a grand opportunity to express love in some form.

Acknowledging that the human experience is all about love, we benefit in (at the very least) these three ways:

1. WE GET TO KNOW OURSELVES

An integral part of the individual journey is to gain self-awareness. When we take a step back and reflect on the events of the day and the role we played in them, we begin to understand ourselves better.

When we look at the various aspects of our lives and observe our participation, however, we must do this from a place of love, not self-hate, anger, or fear. We must be kind to ourselves because showing kindness to yourself is the only way to improve.

When we know better, we do better.

That's how we learn to love ourselves as we are, as well as who we are becoming throughout our journey.

2. WE RECOGNIZE OUR ONENESS

On the deepest level is our connection to all living things. When we dwell in love, we can feel this deep connection. Therefore, we can feel that what we do to another living being, we do to ourselves.

This sense of oneness with humanity, nature, and animals compels us to want that which is for the highest good of all.

Those individuals who are tapped into the energy that flows through all living things are the ones who can, do, and will continue to create a loving existence on the planet.

3. WE SERVE

Every interaction we have is a gift of love. We naturally perform acts of love all day long, smiling and saying "hello" to one another, lending a helping hand, and so on. But we do not realize the impact that these small gestures have on those with whom we are interacting and on humanity as a whole.

When we radiate positive, loving energy,
we pass it along to others,
and they pass it along, and on, and on.

Since we are all connected, what we do for one, we do for all. So whenever you don't think you're making a difference in this world, think again. Each small act of kindness creates a shift and a transformation that resounds in a ripple effect, raising the vibration of the entire planet and every being on it. That's pretty huge, I'd say!

Life is chock full of avenues that allow us to fulfill our purpose for being alive. Every minute of every day we can find ways to learn to love. How great a life purpose is that? We are here, together, now, to learn to love. Enjoy the process!

LET'S TAKE ACTION!
WORKSHEET:

All we need is love

We just learned that the answer to why something happened the way it did is always that you or the person involved is still learning to love.

Can you think back to a time when you didn't know why something happened (A time when you maybe said "why me?!" or "why them?!").

Below, write about the situation and reframe the reason for it happening:

_____

_____

_____

_____

_____

_____

_____

_____

_____

_____

_____

_____

_____

_____

_____

Life Script #31

Worrying vs. Caring
Do You Know the Difference?

Worrying vs. *Caring*
Do You Know the Difference?

— • • • —

Most people would say that worrying is a pointless waste of time and energy. I submit to you that it is actually harmful. Here's why: Worry is fear-based. It is a projection of negative energy. Caring, on the other hand, is a projection of positive energy. When you care about situations or people, you're hoping that things will get better. When you worry about them, you're afraid they won't.

Consider these three reasons you need to quit worrying, starting today:

1. ADDING FUEL TO THE FIRE

When we worry about someone or something, we direct our energy toward the situation. We are, in fact, putting fear and doubt into an already shaky state of affairs.

For instance, maybe you recently found out that a close friend hasn't been feeling well . . . something about a pain in her stomach. So what's the first thing you do? Not that you're a doctor, but you'd probably start contemplating the myriad medical conditions she could have. Then, you call a mutual friend (she's not a doctor, either) and discuss the issue with her. "Cancer? Appendix? Kidneys?"

Then that person goes to the beauty salon and discusses it some more, and those individuals commiserate and worry along with her. Now, how many people have added their energies into the mix?

It's okay to talk about what's going on around you, but try to at least put a positive spin on it, like, "Carol told me she's been having some pain, but I'm sure she'll go see her doctor and it'll all work out just fine. I hope she feels better soon."

Hear the difference?

One approach is called spreading gossip, which is harmful, and the other shows a genuine focus on another person's well-being.

Let's look at the news for a moment. Nowadays, we have twenty-four-hour access to everything that's happening around the world, most of which we can't do anything about. Now, I agree that it's important to be on top of issues of the day, especially when they pertain directly to our lives. But you have to be able to cope with the barrage of information that you're inviting into your home.

I'm sure a number of people out there have become depressed, fearful, and angry from getting an overdose of watching the news day in and day out.

Sometimes we can give too much attention to the "doom and gloom."

There are positive, uplifting news stories also, and we need to start giving more of our mind-space to those. When our collective emotions tilt to the negative, allowing worry, doubt, and fear to set in, at what point are we possibly pulling in more of the same challenges for ourselves?

When more and more people come into agreement about a particular idea, that collective consciousness can become so strong that it creates a self-fulfilling prophecy.

If what we focus our energy on expands and continues to get stronger, then let's try focusing on something good, right?

2. HANGING ON LIKE A DOG WITH A BONE

Sometimes when we're really worried, we hold on to the problem so tightly that we block any kind of resolution from coming in. We end up throwing so much nervous anxiety at an issue that it winds up taking forever to get fixed.

I'm not saying we should all sit around and do nothing when a challenge arises, but I am suggesting that once you take action to get it fixed, don't keep checking on it and asking, "Is it fixed yet? Is it fixed yet? Is it fixed yet?" You have to let go and release it once you set a solution in motion.

If you don't want something to perpetuate and persist, don't give it any energy!

If you do, then, by all means, keep checking. Otherwise, get out of your own way. Go work on something else for a while, and stop thinking about it. Because as soon as you do, the answer to your dilemma will show up, your problem will suddenly be fixed, or "that person" will finally call you back.

3. INTERNALIZING NEGATIVE ENERGY

Did you know that worriers can internalize so many harmful thoughts and feelings that they, in turn, can make themselves ill? When you keep pushing negative energy down into your physical body, that energy can manifest itself and materialize as disease.

Worry, fear, anxiety, anger, resentment, and stress are all toxic to the human body. These emotions will damage your cells. They will literally make you ill if you let them. Being a worrier is a very unhealthy position to put yourself in.

So, do yourself and others a huge favor and quit worrying! Instead, just care. Care about the situation being resolved, care about another person's well-being, and care about yourself. You'll feel so much better, and you'll make others feel a lot better, too. Start today by shutting the door on the things you're afraid of and opening a new door in anticipation of better things to come.

LET'S TAKE ACTION! WORKSHEET:

Three ways to quit worrying today!

1. Adding Fuel to the Fire:

When we worry about someone or something, we direct our energy toward the situation. We are, in fact, putting fear and doubt into an already shaky state of affairs. Armed with your new knowledge, what will you do instead?

2. Hanging on:

If you don't want something to perpetuate and persist, don't give it any energy! Can you think of a time when you were really worried and held on to the problem so tightly that it wound up taking forever to get fixed? Do you think throwing so much nervous anxiety at the issue could have blocked any kind of resolution from coming in?

3. Internalizing Negative Energy:

Did you know that worriers can internalize so many harmful thoughts and feelings that they can make themselves ill?

Rather than Internalizing Negative Energy, what will you now do instead?

"The greatest glory in living
lies not in never falling,
but in rising every time we fall."

-Nelson Mandela

CHAPTER 7

Changing Negatives to *Positives*

Life Script #32

What Your *Negative* Emotions Are Trying To Teach You

What Your *Negative* Emotions Are Trying To Teach You

——— . . . ———

We have emotions for a reason. Negative ones, like anger, aggravation, hurt, and so on, are very important to pay attention to because within them lurks hidden meaning. These emotions are like flashing red lights alerting us that something below the obvious surface has not been dealt with. So the first step is to recognize the purpose of the emotion we are having and understand what is really going on.

It's necessary to realize that we draw to ourselves exactly what we need when we need it in order to grow our consciousness.

As is said, "When the student is ready, the teacher will appear."

Each soul incarnates to meet itself and know itself, specifically in those instances when we feel our strength is being tested. Therefore, through your emotions, you are being brought closer to your true self.

Unresolved issues and unprocessed feelings are being revealed in the experience you are having at that particular moment, but you have to be aware and witness yourself almost as an outsider. This is not to judge yourself. Instead, it is to allow greater love into your being and reality. Those situations are opportunities to elevate your entire life. Emotions are the tools the soul uses for enlightenment. Listen to what they are saying!

Consider this:

Our eyes are not observing our reality, but projecting it.

Thus, the thoughts and feelings we are having on the inside become manifest on the outside.

In other words,
outside reality is aligned with inside reality.

If you are unhappy on the inside, your life circumstances will reflect that, and you will be aligned with what makes you unhappy. This means that if you allow the outside of you to dictate the inside of you, then you will always be a victim of circumstance.

When you have a negative emotion, a need exists to develop your observation and awareness of what you are projecting into your reality, so stop and take notice! This is a golden opportunity for you to dissolve negative attachments, once and for all putting an end to cycles of habits, patterns, and routines that do not serve your highest good. Take advantage of these emotions. They are gifts. Uncovering their roots and reasons will propel you to a much higher vibration.

Now let's take a look at the three hidden agendas of the soul masked as just another foul mood:

1. NOT GOOD ENOUGH

When someone hurts your feelings, it generally makes you feel bad about yourself. These are feelings of inadequacy. Insecurities come flooding out, making us doubt ourselves. Some trait or behavior is being shown to us that we simply do not like.

Don't beat yourself up about it, but do

Take your power back.

What this awareness is meant to teach is that you need to accept yourself just as you are, be kind and compassionate, and believe in yourself. You have exactly what you need in order to be the person you wish to be.

Somewhere along the line, someone made you feel less than, and you are still carrying that pain around with you. It is the same experience playing over and over again but showing up in different forms and scenarios.

2. NOT LOVED

Whether it's a spouse, kids, boss, or even a repairman on whom you were depending, when we need another person to do something for us and they drop the ball, we can become aggravated. Makes sense, right?

But what deep-seated belief about yourself are these "teachers" really poking at?

In your mind, they're saying, "I don't care about you." You think that if they cared about you, they would not have let you down. This is what is causing the aggravation. So the questions you should be asking yourself are: "Do I feel I deserve love?" "Do I love myself?" "Do I feel unloved?"

Recognize that the reality being shown to you reflects a much deeper issue than what appears on the surface. The details of the situation and the people involved may vary, but the underlying reason for the suffering is the same.

3. NOT FREE

Do you find that people are always demanding of your time and attention, which in turn makes you frustrated and angry? When we feel as though we're not being allowed to do the things we want to do or be who we want to be, it feels unnatural to us. Human beings have free will, and when our freedom is being stifled and oppressed, we feel others are holding us back from being fulfilled.

Here is the lesson:

Only you can free yourself.

Know that your journey is not the same as someone else's, no matter how close that person is to you. You were made to move beyond old constructs that hold you back. You'll find that once you release what you've come to expect and have accepted as normal regarding how to live, create, think, and feel, your relationships and work will transform.

Some relationships will end and others will begin. The type of work you do or how you do your work may change. Just remember that anything different is good when breaking old energy and old patterns.

When you understand that changing what's inside alters how you perceive what is happening on the outside, then you have found the keys to the Universe.

*Our thoughts create our reality,
not the other way around.*

So when our reality doesn't look the way we want it to and brings up emotions that are unpleasant to us, that is the message we are being given to start building a bridge between what is and what can be.

*The signs are everywhere
encouraging us to take a chance.*

Taking time to be aware of your reactions, thoughts, and emotions will bring you into a space of clarity and balance. From that vantage point, you can make informed decisions guided and supported by your soul. These decisions will usher in release and healing for you and your life ahead.

LET'S TAKE ACTION! WORKSHEET:

Let's Learn from Our Negative Emotions!

Can you now look at the negative emotions you are feeling from a different perspective? What can you learn from them? What could they be trying to teach you?

_____

_____

_____

_____

_____

_____

_____

_____

_____

_____

_____

_____

_____

Life Script #33

How to Accept and Let Go of People Who Won't Change

How to *Accept* and *Let Go* of People Who Won't Change

———— • • • ————

One of Aesop's Fables tells of a woman who brings a snake that has frozen in the cold back to her home. She makes it warm and cares for it, only to have it bite her when it regains its strength. While dying from the snake's poisonous bite, the bewildered woman asks him how he could do such a thing after she treated him so well and showed him so much kindness?

The snake reminds her that he is a snake and that is what snakes do.

So many times, we want to try to "fix" people who don't want to be "fixed." It may just be in their nature to be the way that they are, even though we know they would be better off with our help. We can get into trouble when we give too much to those who have never asked for our help or who, having asked for it, are likely to take advantage of it.

Have you run into any snakes in your life? Have you allowed someone to take advantage of your kindness or sympathy, or

have you shared your soul with someone not interested in your highest good?

When we have doubts as to whether or not a relationship is truly reciprocal, that is the time to call upon our gifts of intuition and discernment to guide us.

Here are three ways to decipher who in your life will possibly never change and how to deal with them:

1. CROSSING BOUNDARIES

Even if no boundaries have been set, per se,

when you feel uncomfortable in a situation,
then boundaries have been crossed.

So many of us ignore our instincts for the sake of another's. And even when we say "yes" to someone, we're actually screaming "no!" on the inside.

When we internalize our discomfort at a perceived uneven exchange of energy taking place (usually in order to keep the peace and please someone else), we are headed down a very bumpy road.

This behavior is not constructive.

Being tolerant is important when dealing with others, but not if you are worse off for having done it.

We always have options.
We always have the power to choose.

And when we are respectful and speak from the heart, we are never wrong. Therefore, we can express our discomfort and step away; make changes to a situation, if possible, that make it more friendly for us; or accept things completely as they are by considering the source and letting it go.

The issue here is not allowing anyone to take advantage of us. Try to recognize that you always have choices.

You're never required to let someone else
make those choices for you.

2. USE DISCERNMENT, NOT JUDGMENT

When we think someone should change, we have to be careful that we are coming from a place of neutral observation and not a place of arrogance. We are never in a position to know what another person's path is or at what pace they are supposed to move along it.

When we go past observing a person's true nature, whether it appeals to us or not, and begin deeming them unlikeable, unlovable, or unworthy of their right to be on the planet, we are judging, which is always cruel.

Being judgmental is a bad habit that does not contribute to anyone's happiness or joy.

Judging others demonstrates that the "judge" suffers from a lack of self-worth. This is not to say that if someone has on a funny hat or is acting distastefully we won't be inclined to notice. That's just making a simple observation. But complaining about someone's existence is not accepting them as a human being and is an unconscious negative vibration that actually makes you the victim of their actions.

3. POWER OVER OTHERS

There are those people who see life as a fight or competition to gain power or control over others. To them, this is the ultimate measure of success. When you come into contact with people like this, those striving to serve themselves even at the expense of others, the best thing you can do is say to yourself, "He/she is a snake, and that's what snakes do."

On the other end of the spectrum, there are sadly many out there who truly feel they are not meant to go anywhere in life, that they are always meant to be on the losing end, and no matter what you do for them, it will never be enough to get them out of that negative mindset.

Unfortunately, we all have known at least one person who has pulled us down and drained our energy, never taking responsibility for their own life. Again, you may have to step back and stop trying to be so accommodating to those needs or wishes.

The time may come when you realize that you're more committed to their growth and happiness than they are.

When anyone truly commits to changing their life for the better, they will inevitably be challenged to dig deep and rely on their resourcefulness. And that will serve them more than anything you could possibly do.

In both scenarios: the "power over others" and "perpetually powerless" individual may have to be viewed as simply a different sort of animal. It could be that their assessment of themselves is part of their makeup and is nothing you can change.

Just know that if someone says or does something that makes you feel that a line has been crossed—then it has. And once you recognize that, even if it's awkward or difficult to do so, you need to put your needs above theirs.

Be who you are and treat everyone along your path with dignity and respect. You will be freer and happier if you let go and accept others for who they are and how they choose to be.

LET'S TAKE ACTION! WORKSHEET:

Will they change?

We can get into trouble when we give too much to those who have never asked for our help or who, having asked for it, are likely to take advantage of it. Have you allowed someone to take advantage of your kindness or sympathy? If so, reflect on it below using the three ways to decipher who in your life will possibly never change and how to deal with them:

_____

_____

_____

_____

_____

_____

_____

_____

_____

_____

_____

_____

_____

Life
Script
#34

Why You're
Having Trouble
Moving On

Why You're Having Trouble
Moving On

--- • • • ---

Moving forward in life can be a daunting proposition. It can feel quite uncomfortable finding yourself at the start of a new chapter of your personal evolution. But why is that? Is it fear of change? Self-doubt? Difficulty breaking old patterns? As a matter of fact, it can encompass all three of these issues.

If we take a closer look at the reasons we have trouble detaching from the past and proceeding into unknown territory, we can gain clarity and shift our perspective to seeing change as a grand opportunity.

Here are three things to consider that may be holding you back from moving forward:

1. WE BECOME ADDICTED TO THE PAIN AND SUFFERING

It sounds irrational, but in many cases, our emotional pain is like a drug. It can provide a temporary high, an escape from reality. It's a way in which we can distract ourselves from dealing with the challenges of life and facing the truth.

Suffering and negative drama can, in a strange capacity, feel like a close friend on whom you can rely.

In addition, our built-in critical voice is always there to support us whenever we consciously or unconsciously give our power away to negativity and take on the role of victim. At times, being critical of ourselves and placing limits on what is possible can feel safer than exploring who we fundamentally are, which is often a scary truth to explore.

But not a single one of us should be afraid or ashamed of who we are. Yes, we will say and do things that do not represent our best self now and then. We will feel unloved and unloving at times. But each and every one of us has a special and precious light inside. So be proud of who you are. You are beautiful and can't fail. Stop calling every hurdle or misstep a failure! You can only learn, grow, and have more experiences.

2. WE KEEP LOOKING FOR VALIDATION WE'RE NEVER GOING TO GET

The biggest mistake many of us make is that we look for someone else to give us self-worth. And it always turns out the same—disappointment.

Anytime we give another person control over our happiness and how we feel about ourselves, we're in trouble.

Nothing good can or will ever come of it. No one else is responsible for our self-worth, and because of self-doubt (which is always lurking in the back of our minds), this is a tough concept to accept.

It's difficult to keep ourselves from pointing at another person and blaming them for our unhappiness.

The good news is, once you recognize that no one has control over your life or your feelings about yourself, you're liberated. You experience freedom when you become aware that no one else's existence or opinion takes precedence over your own.

What anyone else says or does has no bearing on the strength and beauty inherent inside of you. So the reality is that no person or circumstance can cause harm to the love and honor you hold for yourself—unless you allow it.

3. WE CLING TO THE OLD AND FAMILIAR

Many of us get into the habit of doing the same things over and over again.

*It's comfortable. It's convenient.
But that's how we become
stuck, stagnant, and complacent.*

We get used to assuming the worst instead of assuming the best, so we become attached to old energies that have no interest in serving our highest good.

Our unwillingness to let go ultimately produces the gradual construction of a mental wall, one we build to hold in all of our tired, worn out, negative thinking from the past. Tearing down that wall, one negative thought at a time, then allows us to see the abundant possibilities shimmering on the other side.

The only way to get out of this rut is to be here NOW!

*Where you are at this very moment is
all that truly matters and all that truly exists.*

The past is a memory, and the future hasn't happened yet (and is constantly subject to change), so you can only receive in the present.

Notice that a gift is called a present. The energy of your greatest good is blocked because you are not living in the present moment where the infinite dwells. Energy is a current that is currently flowing in and out,

*so if your thoughts are focused elsewhere,
in the past or future, then you are never in a
position to meet and receive in the Now.*

What's happening is that in every moment, we are all being guided toward our greatest good. That may mean a significant period in life must end because we have learned all there is to learn from it and are simply ready for the next step in our journey.

Life is filled with endings and beginnings.
When one stage of life concludes,
it's only to make room for a more appropriate
and profound journey to begin.

Never think that you've wasted months or years in a relationship or a job or some other situation that didn't turn out the way you had hoped. You are always exactly where you are supposed to be. No experience is ever wasted. There is meaning and purpose in each moment of your life if you allow yourself to see it clearly.

So just know that it's safe to welcome the new and different into your life with open arms. You have the ability to do so, and once you do, you'll be freer, stronger, wiser, and happier than you've ever been before.

LET'S TAKE ACTION! WORKSHEET:

Let's find out why you can't move on...

Is there a specific situation from which you are having trouble moving on? If so, ask yourself...

1) Have I Become Addicted to the Pain and Suffering?

Can you think of a time when you were kept from moving on because you were addicted to the pain and suffering of a certain situation? How will you recognize this next time and what will you do differently?

_____

_____

2) Do I Keep Looking for Validation I'm Never Going to Get?

Have you given another person control over your happiness and how you feel about yourself?

_____

_____

3) Am I Clinging to the Old and Familiar?

Are you simply acting from the habit of doing the same things over and over again? Are you clinging to this situation because it's comfortable? Is it too scary to let go?

_____

_____

Keep it up: What can you do every day to keep yourself in the present moment?

Life
Script
#35

If You *Multitask*
Get Ready for the
Consequences

If You *Multitask* Get Ready for the Consequences

———— • • • ————

Most people think running around as fast as they can, trying to get things done, and doing multiple tasks at once results in more efficiency and productivity. But many people would be surprised to learn that they are ultimately creating inefficiency and lack of productivity.

Impossible? Well, ask yourself how many details you overlook and wrong decisions you make when you're on turbo speed. Then, ask yourself how much time it takes you to go back and correct all of the errors that were made.

The fact is that we accomplish a lot less when we're in a hurry and dividing our attention between several different tasks at the same time.

The reason for this can easily be explained from an energetic point of view.

You would naturally assume that the faster you're going, the faster your energy vibration, right? So, you must be attracting the same higher vibration as the things around you, in alignment with happiness, peace, joy, and general ease of flow to your life. But that's not the way it works.

The truth is that when our bodies and minds operate at a breakneck pace, we experience it on a frequency that is low and slow. This means that we align ourselves with other emotions that are of a low vibration, like anger, fear, worry, and frustration.

When we're rushing around and not being mindful of our thoughts and actions, we create more of what we're trying to avoid. This is when mistakes happen, decisions are poor, and nothing seems to go right.

Take several moments throughout your day and ask yourself if you feel centered or off-balance. If you feel centered, then you're calm, in control of your emotions, and aware of everything that's happening around you. In this state, you're able to handle each task efficiently.

If you feel off-balance, then you're scattered, stressed out, and everything you touch turns into a big mess. One thing goes wrong, then another, then another until you wish you hadn't gotten out of bed!

When you do feel yourself drifting during the day, here are some ways you can raise your vibration by slowing down, allowing you to accomplish twice as much while experiencing a more peaceful, productive life:

1. STOP IN YOUR TRACKS

Whatever you're frantically doing, no matter what it is, you need to stop immediately. If you don't, you're headed down a slippery slope.

Nothing good can come from frantic energy.

You are just asking for trouble. Know that whatever it is you are doing will get done when, and if, it's meant to get done. Recognize that you have been thrown off-balance and need to collect yourself and get centered before you unwittingly pull in negative circumstances.

2. STEP OUT OF THE ROOM

If there are people around you, there is a distinct possibility that you are picking up on their energy, which may be carrying with it all kinds of issues that they are having at the moment.

Step out of the room to break the energy, close your eyes, take a deep breath, and imagine yourself with white light surrounding you like a shield. This will create in you the intention of being your own sovereign entity protected from absorbing that energy off of others.

3. TRUST LIFE

Trust and have faith that everything works out the way it's supposed to and that you don't need to control every detail of a situation.

Believe me, life will go on and time will pass whether you're in charge or not.

Have faith that all will happen in its own time and that you will get where you're going at exactly the perfect moment.

Be sure to remember that when your mind and body are flying around, so to speak, be aware that it's happening and take a breath. Because at that moment, you are choosing your alignment, your point of attraction to all things. Simply taking action to be calm and mindful will attract to you the clearest solution and/or most efficient outcome in everything you do.

LET'S TAKE ACTION! WORKSHEET:

Centering Check-In Challenge

It's important to check in with yourself a few times a day. Simply taking action to be calm and mindful will attract to you the clearest solution and/or most efficient outcome in everything you do. Try to do this check-in three times a day for a week:

How do I feel right now?
(Choose one)

Centered? (calm, in control of your emotions, and aware of everything that's happening around you.)

Describe how you feel:

or

Off-balance? (scattered, stressed out, running around at full speed and everything you touch turns into a big mess.)

Describe how you feel:

Then keep it up!! You're doing great! Check in again later!

Then you have 3 action options - Do one or all three!:

1.
Stop in your tracks!

How did this make you feel?

2.
Step Out of the Room.

How did this make you feel?

3.
Trust Life.

How did this make you feel?

Life Script #36

Criticizing Others Is More Harmful Than You Think

Criticizing Others Is More Harmful Than You Think

———— . . . ————

Have you ever noticed how some people don't think twice before criticizing someone else? Or how their tolerance level for ideas that are different from their own is practically nonexistent, making them argumentative and easily angered? Well, the truth is, there will always be differences between human beings. And since I don't want to criticize those who criticize, I'll preface this article by suggesting that if those people realized they were being so negative, they would alter their behavior as soon as it came to their attention. At least, that's my hopeful assumption.

My goal here is merely to point out that if all is interconnected, meaning everything affects everything else, then perhaps

we need to investigate why it's so important to consciously choose where we put our attention and how we spend our time.

Are we finding fault with situations and tearing people down or lifting them up and encouraging their healing?

Let's take a look at three ways in which the act of criticism creates a destructive force of energy that reaches much further than we might imagine:

1. NEGATIVE ENERGY

When you throw negative energy at another human being, you're hurting him or her, whether you realize it or not. You have the ability to interfere with their self-esteem and self-worth, which changes who they are and how they perceive the world around them. At the same time, you are throwing negative energy out into the Universe for yourself. What you put out is what you get back.

Would you want someone to do or say something to hurt you? Of course not! Be nice. Be mature. Let's not forget the Golden Rule. Everyone makes mistakes. Mistakes are necessary tools of wisdom and growth. If you truly feel that someone is wrong, then don't give them any energy at all. Focusing your attention on the perceived insult only gives it more power.

2. PSYCHOLOGY 101

When you make derogatory statements about others,
the centered people in the room
know exactly who you're really talking about:
yourself!

When an individual lashes out at another, it's a defense mechanism. Their behavior is a product of feelings and issues they're trying to cope with that have nothing to do with the other person.

This behavior makes them appear "less than." They are announcing to others that they are not centered and that there is an imbalance of harmony in their life that requires blame to be placed somewhere, anywhere other than at their own doorstep.

Ego is at work here, and whenever the ego takes over, you can rest assured it's not going to create a positive experience.

The ego only looks out for number one, self-centered,
not centered-in-self.

Big difference!

Respect yourself by respecting others. Honor and love yourself and you will never dishonor or hate another.

3. COLLECTIVE CONSCIOUSNESS

Are you adding to the awareness, enlightenment, and evolution of humanity by acting in a way that raises the vibration of the planet as a whole, or are you sending us backward by fueling lower-vibrational energy? Let's set a positive example for our children, as they are the future of the human race.

Yes, we still have wars. Yes, we still witness injustices. No one is immune to feeling sympathy for the suffering that goes on in the world. So the question then becomes, are you one to perpetuate these issues by spending your time and attention choosing thoughts and words of anger and dissension, or do you spend your time trying to elevate the planet by uplifting others and inspiring hope for a peaceful future?

Anger begets anger. Violence begets violence. That's why there is so much pain in the world.

But we should never be accepting of behavior that blatantly harms another human being.

So for those who profess to stand strongly against the atrocities of mankind, put your passion to work by doing all that you can to come from a place of love.

Be of service to those in need of help. Don't come from a place of anger toward their situation and hate for their oppressors. If you engage in the latter, all you are doing is simply adding strength and momentum to the energies you claim to be fighting against. That only perpetuates the endless cycle.

We can't solve the world's issues with the same mindset that created them.

It is our pure and loving intentions, devoid of ego, that will unfailingly support the highest good of all.

Each personal shift in self-awareness and act of focus on what's good and positive - no matter how small it may seem - assists and supports the transformation of the entire planet.

This is an active role that we can all fulfill individually with dramatic collective results. When you don't feel like you've found your purpose in life, remember that.

Your reason for being on this planet, however it manifests and through whatever medium you choose to express it, is to be consciously aware of radiating love and kindness from your being. This is in order to teach by example and contribute to the expansion of a harmonious unity consciousness. And the most important and far-reaching changes are those you make within.

Humanity is interconnected. We are each part of the whole. There is no separation. What you do to another, you do to yourself and the planet. What affects one person does indeed affect us all. We are not powerless to change the world. Every single human being is significant and has the power to make the world a better place.

Let's concentrate on that energy, the energy we want to increase, not on the negative energy we see in the world. Some say that violence and suffering are the reality and criticize others for not appearing painfully aware of it. I say that because we are aware of it, we must strive to create a new reality. We need to stop reinforcing and feeding the old, painful one. Even the smallest positive contribution is truly meaningful and causes a shift in the right direction.

We know that we're all different, have our own opinions, and that not everyone is going to agree on everything. Having said that, the bottom line is as it has always been. If you can't say something nice . . . Well, you know the rest.

"You are not a drop in the ocean.
You are the entire ocean, in a drop."
- Rumi

LET'S TAKE ACTION! WORKSHEET:

Collective Consciousness Self-Reflection:

Are you adding to the awareness, enlightenment, and evolution of humanity by acting in a way that raises the vibration of the planet as a whole, or are you sending us backward by fueling lower-vibrational energy?

Are you one to perpetuate issues by spending your time and attention choosing thoughts and words of anger and dissension, or do you spend your time trying to elevate the planet by uplifting others and inspiring hope for a peaceful future?

Reflect below...

Life
Script
#37

Why Attacks on the
Innocent Do the *Opposite*
of What They Intend

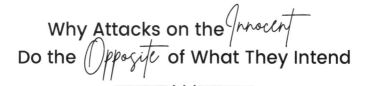

Why Attacks on the Innocent Do the Opposite of What They Intend

· · ·

The evil people in this world have but one goal, and that is to make the good people of this world suffer. Now they may, for a time, instill fear and sadness. However, what are the real effects of their evil acts?

The real effects are not even understood by those individuals who manifest the evil because they cannot see past their own hate and misery.

They are unable to see that their efforts only serve to backfire and ultimately thwart them in their mission.

We know in our hearts that what was meant for our harm will always be used in our favor. And so, when evildoers perpetrate unspeakable crimes against us, this is what they are actually doing, not to us, but to themselves:

1. THEY EXPOSE WHO THEY REALLY ARE

They want the civilized world to pay attention to them, but when they get our attention, they lose big time! Their arrogance is their downfall. They are their own worst enemies. They bring their dark ways into the light to be clearly seen. And once seen, that cruelty will brand them.

2. THEY CREATE A BACKLASH

Universal Law is quite clear. What you put out reflects back like a mirror. If you intentionally harm an innocent soul, be it a person, animal, or the planet, guess what is going to happen to you?

There is always a balancing of energy taking place. Thus, the more negative, dark energy one creates, the more that energy will be reciprocated in kind.

Likewise, good will always receive more good, which means those who are evil can never win, because they bring the evil they do back on themselves like a *boomerang.*

3. THEY WAKE A SLEEPING GIANT

They do not expect us to replace our temporary fears with a deep-seated, fierce love for humanity. Our boundless determination to live in a loving, free world (in stark contrast to the type of world the evil ones support) is ignited in us like wildfire.

When we witness the suffering of others, we come together as one.

We see ourselves as human beings on the deepest level. We feel compassion to the core of our souls and unite in strength beyond measure.

The time is now when humanity is saying, "Enough is enough!" The time is now for the good people of this planet to create so much light that the darkness has nowhere to go. And we can do just that. Make no mistake about it. Light is designed to extinguish darkness. That's what light does.

LET'S TAKE ACTION! WORKSHEET:

The Negative Energy Backlash

Can you think of some examples of times when attacks on the innocent (that you witnessed personally or you have heard about throughout history) actually ended up making things worse for the attacker? Did it expose who they really are, wake a sleeping giant or create a backlash?

"When you reach the end of your rope,
tie a knot in it and hang on."

-Franklin D. Roosevelt

CHAPTER 8

Facing
Challenges

Life Script #38

Frustration and How To Cope

.

Frustration and How to 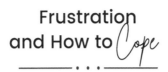 Cope

───── • • • ─────

All frustration stems from a lack of understanding.

It may be concerning a particular situation or a person's behavior or choices. We feel worried, in a hurry, and out of control concerning whatever it is that is not "going well." But all that our emotions do at this point is send out to the Universe agitated energy that only serves to block the resolution we desire.

Let's examine four questions we ask ourselves at those seemingly unbearable moments of frustration in order to cope with them and gain some level of clarity:

1. WHY IS THIS HAPPENING?

Whether you are late getting to an appointment, your son fails his driving test, or your flight gets canceled, you must recognize that something unforeseen is going on here. Perhaps you and your teenager were meant to avoid dangerous situations while driving at a certain moment, or the person you were meant to meet while sitting and waiting for the next flight turns out to be your soul mate.

Never rush and never be disappointed that a situation isn't going smoothly. It is undoubtedly a blessing in disguise. There are no random acts. There is always meaning even if you do not see it, so try not to waste your energy taking issue with whatever happens.

Just go with the flow.

2. HOW COULD YOU DO THAT?

Something not being done the way we want it done, or someone not doing what we want them to do can be a real challenge. Frustration builds up inside of us like a pot of water about to boil over. The circumstances make absolutely no sense to us.

We analyze how this could be possible, then rack our brains trying to figure out how to alter or rectify the situation. What we have to stop and realize is that there are creative solutions, opportunities, and people that get brought in to "save the day." You may never see it coming!

When one person drops the ball or screws up (however you want to put it), it's because you are being shown that the situation isn't meant to continue going in that particular direction. You are meant to have a much better experience than reality is currently presenting to you.

This is why chaos has to ensue once in a while, to break ties with the old and bring in the new.

So, when something looks like a disaster, know that it's because something fantastic will show up on its heels!

3. WHAT IS THE ANSWER?

I'm sure you've anxiously awaited an important phone call, all the while saying to yourself, "Why haven't they called yet? What is taking so long? When are they going to call?"

This is a perfect example of giving something too much energy.

Obsessing about a situation with needless chatter delays its progress. If you quit thinking about it, answers will come. The phone will ring or something else will happen that takes care of the issue.

Understand that at frustrating moments such as these, you are being taught patience and the art of allowing and letting go. It isn't easy to surrender to the possibilities of the unknown, but you will receive your answer one way or another.

Taking your mind off of things and waiting a bit isn't the end of the world. If you do, you'll be amazed how quickly and perfectly everything falls into place, perhaps even better than you could have imagined.

4. WHERE IS THIS GOING?

Life is a process. Trust it. The day-to-day, hour-to-hour happenings taking place in your life may appear completely unrelated on the surface, but in truth, an orchestrated, interlocking chain of events is occurring.

Human nature is such that we always want to know what is going on and why, but we don't always need to know. Even in times of major upheaval and turmoil,

understand that everything is part of a necessary process, and after the dust settles, the outcome will reveal itself.

When we decide that having answers that we haven't yet accessed is imperative, frustration sets in. We suffer through feelings of anxiety and aggravation because we have not yet mastered patience, acceptance, and trust.

Granted, it's no easy feat to accomplish those things. But when we grasp the fact that we can never know everything, that so many things are not meant for our understanding at the particular moment of our choosing, we can finally live in a place of inner peace without any doubt of the perfection of our experiences.

LET'S TAKE ACTION! WORKSHEET:

Mantras for Replacing Frustration

All frustration stems from a lack of understanding. When frustration occurs, practice replacing your disempowering questions with these mantras to help gain some level of clarity:

① "WHY IS THIS HAPPENING?" ⟶ "Go with the flow"

② "HOW COULD YOU DO THAT?" ⟶ "Something fantastic will show up"

③ "WHAT IS THE ANSWER?" ⟶ "Surrender to the possibilities of the unknown"

④ "WHERE IS THIS GOING?" ⟶ "Life is a process. Trust it."

The next time you feel frustration, come back to this page and try these replacements to help you cope.

Life Script #39

Who Has Been *Pushing* Your Buttons

Who Has Been *Pushing* Your Buttons

———— • • • ————

From time to time, we all get our buttons pushed by the people in our lives. This can be anyone with whom we interact, whether a relative, friend, coworker, or life partner, it doesn't matter. When they hurt your feelings, make you angry, or repeatedly do something or behave in some way that drives you up the wall, those buttons are pushed.

Sometimes, we don't even know we have buttons!

But when we let other people poke at the metaphorical control panel that is our emotions, we have a choice:

To react or respond.

The difference between reacting and responding is a matter of who is holding the power. When we go into reactive mode, our behavior is automatic and either defensive or offensive. The result is a loss of control over our thoughts and emotions. We are no longer in charge of our feelings and have permitted others to strip away our personal power and sense of self, along with our happiness.

However, when we go into a responsive mode, our behavior is based on an awareness of who we have allowed to push our buttons and why. The result of this understanding is a calmer, more effective approach, which vastly increases our chances of living a more centered life. We come away from those encounters more tolerant of others and at peace with ourselves.

So if you want to take your power back and begin to deactivate your buttons, consider these three steps that will take you from powerless to powerful:

1. USE YOUR IMAGINATION

Sometimes life gets away from us and we become complacent, falling into a limited routine. We get tunnel vision, seeing only one possible way of viewing our circumstances.

When this happens, we often give life's unexpected challenges undeserved significance.

Using our minds as creative tools, we can make circumstances appear larger or smaller, depending on how much focus, energy, and importance we place on them.

Picture a huge bubble looming over your head. It's so big because you've been thinking about it and thinking about it, blowing it up bigger and bigger. This huge bubble is filled with the insensitive selfish behavior of someone else, which has taken ownership of your peace and joy. You are at its mercy as it weighs heavily atop your head. You feel as though you're the size of an ant, powerless as it presses down on you.

Now picture yourself as a mighty, powerful giant. We're talking a thousand times the size of this bubble. The tables have turned as you now tower over it. You realize how it could never have any effect on you, so you step on it and crush it like a grape.

From this vantage point, you can see far and wide. The view is amazing! There was so much you were missing: unlimited choices, endless options, and not a tunnel in sight!

Pull out your imagination. Dust it off. Open up your vision. You'll find a whole world just waiting for you out there, a world full of solutions, ideas, and inspiration.

The only one powerful enough to hold you back is you.

2. LET YOUR HEART DECIDE

We all rely much too heavily on our heads to make decisions, and most of the time, we wish we hadn't. I don't care what our heads tell us we should or shouldn't do, can or cannot have, need, want, expect, know, or don't know.

If it doesn't feel right in your heart, then it isn't the right direction for you.

Our feelings are our barometer.

They are what we need to rely on to forge our path in life. When we feel fear, anger, anxiety, sadness, or any other emotion that makes us feel bad, our hearts are alerting us to the fact that we have given our power away to someone or something that has no right to it.

Whenever you put your happiness in the hands of another, red flags should be everywhere! That is not who you are. You are strong and rational. You are not the victim of needless suffering.

Rely on your heart. It will pump courage into you so you can see beyond the fear, anger, sadness, etc. and choose to respond differently. You may not know where your heart will ultimately lead you, but what really matters is deciding to take that leap of faith and trust it.

3. PLANT YOUR GARDEN

How does your garden grow? You plant seeds in your garden every day, giving life to thoughts, words, and actions for the future. Observing aspects of your life today will shed light on whatever you have planted and nurtured for years.

Do you notice the plants that you've nourished have flourished, and the seeds that have grown are the ones you've been watering? Have you tended to situations or people that steal your joy and knock you off-balance?

If the answer is "yes," then begin today to be a more diligent gardener. Encourage what you've planted to thrive, and allow any unwelcome undergrowth to wither away by not giving it your energy and attention. "Weeds" do not please you or serve your greatest good. Instead, choose to plant seeds of awareness, understanding, and peace. If you do, you'll be able to watch the brilliance of all the many colors begin to bloom in the garden of your life.

From day to day, we are tested. Whether in our professional or personal lives, those around us will push our buttons and challenge us in one way or another. By choosing to react to certain individuals and situations, giving them control over our personal power and sense of self, we are waiving our right to a life of peace and happiness.

Reflecting upon why we have given certain people the power to push our buttons, and noticing the types of situations that cause us to react rather than respond allow us to gain crucial awareness. And that awareness alone will begin the "button deactivation process."

Where are your buttons? Who has a finger on them? Whatever the issue at hand, say to it, "You no longer have control over me! I'm taking my power back from you!"

How does it feel to take your power back? Empowering!

LET'S TAKE ACTION! WORKSHEET:

Reactive vs. Responsive

Whats the difference between reactive mode and responsive mode? Which one is more powerful and why?

_____

_____

_____

Think of a situation in which you acted in reactive mode and there was a negative outcome. What happened?

_____

_____

_____

In that same situation, how could you have changed your reactive response into a responsive response instead? What do you think would have been the outcome?

_____

_____

_____

Next time you feel yourself slipping into reactive mode, what 3 steps will you take to get into responsive mode instead?

1) _____

2) _____

3) _____

Life Script #40

The Roles Fear Plays in Our Lives

The Roles *Fear*
Plays in Our Lives

— • • • —

Fears we face in the external world are actually providing insight into our internal world. If we listen to fear's messages, we can turn what appears to be negative into a positive experience by allowing fear to help us recognize the moment it comes into our lives and why.

Fear has a purpose. Its purpose in your life may be different from its purpose in another's, but it is always useful if we take advantage of what it is trying to teach us.

Consider these three important roles fear plays in each of our lives and how we can work with it in positive ways:

1. FEAR AS A HEALER

Healing can take many forms and have many healers. Believe it or not, fear is one of them. When you experience a fearful situation over and over again, the fear is trying to get your attention. The situation is going to keep coming up until the fear that it evokes is gone.

Feelings of fear arise to the surface in order to bring to our attention the places inside of us that need recognition.

As soon as we become aware of this phenomenon, we can utilize fear as a motivator to move us beyond the situation that is causing it, and hence, move beyond the fear once and for all.

A positive and profound way to do this is to approach every aspect of your life with a childlike sense of wonder, having no preconceived notions or assumptions of how your life can work.

2. FEAR AS A CREATOR

We have been given free will to help create our realities. Most of the time, without even realizing it, we do so through our fearfulness. Fear of not having something will create its absence, while fear of having something will create its presence. Many people live in fear of both.

Some may argue that fear of being in danger helps us to avoid hazardous situations, but I think that putting energy into avoiding situations that you fear draws those very experiences to you. And I believe it is our intuition, that little voice inside our head, not fear, that helps us avoid danger . . . when we listen to it, that is.

3. FEAR AS A COMFORTER

Ironically, fear can be quite comforting to some. When one has felt fear of something for a long time, their attachment to it becomes natural to them. This familiar energy feels normal.

Fear can act as an escape, a hiding place, a retreat from the unknown.

It can distort one's perception to the point where fear can feel safer than living life to the fullest. Freedom can be quite scary, so retreating in fear may bring comfort.

No emotion, be it positive or negative, is ever wasted. There is always a purpose behind it. It is our job as human beings to figure out what that purpose is. So next time you feel fear, truly feel it, asking yourself what role it is meant to play in your life at that moment. You may just discover invaluable information about yourself in the process.

LET'S TAKE ACTION! WORKSHEET:

Let's Face Your Fears!

What fear have you overcome and how did you overcome it?

_____

_____

_____

_____

_____

_____

_____

_____

What fear do you still want to overcome but haven't been able to yet? What do you think is holding you back and why?

_____

_____

_____

_____

_____

_____

_____

_____

Life Script #41

Breaking Free
from *Anger*

Breaking Free from
Anger
_____.⒜._____

No matter how badly we all want to be happy, much of the time we feel a whirlpool-like force pulling us back into negative and destructive emotional patterns. No matter how desperately we want to break free and stop spinning in circles, we simply can't. The force is magnetic and much too strong. The power of the subconscious mind is formidable and will do everything it can to keep us in its grasp.

Releasing and letting go of those deep-seated beliefs that do not serve our highest good allows us to inch far enough away so that we may begin to move in another direction. And a fresh direction is the only way to ever break this endless cycle.

Little by little, by getting farther and farther out of the reach of that magnetic pull, it will lose more and more of its power and hold on us. That's the only way to free ourselves from this invisible prison.

Following these three suggestions will help you swim out of that dangerous whirlpool of anger, resentment, disgust, and feelings of insufficiency (not enough money, not enough affection, not thin enough, not smart enough, not enough whatever) in your life.

1. REPROGRAM YOUR SUBCONSCIOUS MIND

Everyone has memories of past hurts and old wounds. These are attachments that hold you back and block your highest good. They have programmed into you a learned response either from your upbringing or environment or both.

That is not who you are. Holding on to past disappointments and hurts is robbing you of your power in the present, and is also creating your future.

To release these old energies and make room for new reservoirs to enter in, the subconscious mind has to be reprogrammed. This can be done by listening to subliminal suggestions and guided meditations in musical recordings, such as those from Brain Sync, Hemi-Sync and others.

This positive reinforcement will eventually replace the negative tape in your head that plays over and over again, the one that's keeping you living in the past and not moving forward. In addition, saying to yourself,

"I am happy. I am healthy. I am free,"

and many other affirmations you can think of will eventually change the negative labels you have placed on yourself. Start labeling yourself in a good way.

This won't change your thoughts overnight, but stick with it, and you WILL see yourself in a new, more positive light. Once you begin believing differently about yourself and your life, the world around you will shift in your favor. Do the work. Face the fact that change, freedom, and happiness come from within.

2. BE "BORN YESTERDAY"

If you're sick of the way things are in your life and don't like the way you feel, rewrite The Book of You. Start today! Create a new beginning with new possibilities. As the adage goes, "Today is the first day of the rest of your life." Make each one count.

You are not your past.
Reinvent yourself.
When the sun comes up in the morning,
it is another chance at a fresh start.
Do something powerful with it!

3. FORGIVE

Forgiving another person, a situation, and especially yourself may be the hardest, most important, profound thing you ever do. It will also bring the greatest rewards.

Internalizing anger and resentment toward yourself or someone else is a heavy burden that can consume your life. You may be happy in every aspect except for that one person who has hurt you deeply. It's that one thing you can't seem to get over. You desperately want to forget it, but that undertow keeps pulling you back into the whirlpool. You can't seem to escape no matter how hard you try.

The bottom line is that you have to come to the point where you have suffered enough. Your children have suffered enough. Your spouse has suffered enough. When you are no longer vibrating that negative energy, you will see a remarkable shift in you and those around you. It will be almost immediate. Make a command decision that enough is enough.

It's exhausting to internalize anger, and doing so for prolonged periods can damage the very cells in your body, making you weak or physically ill.

That which you embrace has no power over you. You are empowered by forgiving and letting go.

Be respectful of the choices other people make in their lives. They may be different from yours, but all experiences serve a higher purpose.

End the cycle of anger in your life. It's time to live in peace and joy and feel relief. A huge burden will be taken off your shoulders. It's the ultimate act of self-love. It's time.

 # LET'S TAKE ACTION!
WORKSHEET:

Let your anger go!

Is there a whirlpool of anger, resentment, disgust, or feelings of insufficiency (not enough money, not enough affection, not thin enough, not smart enough, not enough whatever) swimming around in your heart somewhere?

What is it? Describe it on the next two pages – get it ALL out once and for all! Pour out your feelings and emotions about it!

Then we are going to LET IT GO! Take that page, tear it out, rip it up and throw it away – and symbolically along with it, your anger about the situations.

Get it All Out! →

Keep going! →

Let it Out!

Now tear this out, rip it up and throw your anger away!
Let it go and free yourself!

Life Script #42

Why Some People Totally *Annoy* You

Why Some People Totally Annoy You

You can be the most enlightened, loving, open-minded person on the planet and STILL get annoyed by some people. Don't feel guilty about your feelings and don't try to internalize them in order to keep the peace.

There are three positive and understandable reasons why you can be a beacon of spiritual growth, and yet, not like everybody, at the same time:

1. YOUR HIGHER VIBRATION

The challenge you may face with certain people is that they vibrate differently than you. It is a physical reaction that can feel like the shrill of nails scraping down a chalkboard. It's the other person's energy that is making you uncomfortable. In turn, this is also why you automatically "click" with certain people right away. You're vibrating on the same level.

Go by your feelings and intuition. It's okay to not be around particular individuals, sharing the same physical space with them. And if you have to be (because it's a family member or work associate or the like), remember that removing yourself from the room is always an option.

2. YOUR PERSONAL POWER

The difference between you and another person can be a matter of personal power.

Power lies in our words and actions in the present moment.
If those around us are living in the past or the future,
then they may easily be an annoyance.

When a person is stuck in the past or constantly worried about the future, they have a tendency to moan and groan and complain about their life and take on the role of "victim."

But when you use your personal power, you instinctively know that you are being given two options: to speak up and take a positive stand in the hopes of changing something you don't like OR to accept whatever it is and move on. Conversely, those individuals who come from a place of raw, uncontrolled emotion get nowhere beyond upsetting those around them and pulling in more negative energy for themselves.

3. YOUR POSITIVE VISION

You are more than likely a free-thinking, non-discriminatory, non-judgmental person who is open to possibilities, since you're reading this book. You know that positive thoughts create positive results, while negative thoughts create negative results, and that you always have the power to choose.

When you are presented with the views of another that are negative and closed-minded, recognize that they are choosing that life experience for themselves. It has nothing to do with you. All knowledge is a form of light, and they simply aren't able to see the bigger picture just yet. It's all about awareness.

So remember, next time someone says or does something that annoys you, do yourself a huge favor and take it with a grain of salt.

LET'S TAKE ACTION! WORKSHEET:

Annoyed?

Are there some people in your life that just annoy you? Instead of feeling guilty about it or internalizing it in order to keep the peace, write down which of the three reasons mentioned in this chapter are at play and how you can avoid the negative feelings:

Life
Script
📋 #43

Need an *Attitude* Adjustment?
Here's How to Get One

Need an *Attitude* Adjustment?
Here's How to Get One

————— • • • —————

One day you wake up feeling irritated by everyone, focused on "what's wrong" in your life, or just plain apathetic to all of it. This cranky disposition just crept up on you. You may stay in this mood for a while, but eventually say to yourself,

"I hate feeling this way! This is not who I am. I need an attitude adjustment!"

Consider for a moment the possibility that you didn't just fall into your bad mood based on a single event but that

you gradually became immersed in a lack of happy thoughts due to an absorption of negative energy from the people around you.

Perhaps a coworker made an unflattering remark to you the other day and you've been trying to think of a comeback ever since. Maybe a friend called four times in the past week to vent about how her husband is a jerk and her kids don't appreciate her, and trying to be a good friend, you make her feel better by listening to every sordid detail. Then you recall for her examples in your own life when loved ones were insensitive to you as well.

The effects of these incidents may not be immediately noticeable, but each one builds upon the one before it until they attach to you and take hold.

What this means from an energetic point of view is that little by little, your vibrational level has dipped to where you are feeling the shift. It is so subtle sometimes that you don't even realize it until it's too late and it has affected your attitude in a big way.

Your thoughts increasingly grow overly negative from day to day, gaining in momentum, until finally, you've had enough! As far as you're concerned, you are unloved and unappreciated, and no one is going to convince you any differently.

So what do we do when we realize we are the guest of honor at our own pity party? Here are three tried-and-true solutions to help you begin feeling like your cheery self again:

1. THE HAPPINESS CATALOG

The Happiness Catalog is where you write down all of the things you enjoy. For instance, you may list: playing your guitar (which you haven't made time to do in years), taking a bubble bath, going out to the movies, or taking your dog for a long walk while the sun shines brightly on your face. Or how about baking cookies, putting together a puzzle on the kitchen table, or dancing around the house to your favorite tunes? Maybe you love flowers. Go to the market and buy your favorite kind and just stare at them all day, if you want. This idea is akin to looking through a seed catalog full of beautiful, colorful options that are just perfect for you.

Personal happiness can only come from the experience of joy. No one can do it for you.

It has to come from feeling good on the inside. An imbalance in one's life caused by an abundance of negativity and a lack of fun and play will eventually manifest into a bad attitude that will be a challenge to shake off. Put balance back into your life by doing things that make you smile.

2. NOTE TO SELF

Try this experiment: sit down and have your "future self" write a letter to your "current self." Use your imagination and fantasize! The sky's the limit! Tell your "current self" how amazing life is! The "future you" is having the time of her/his life! The "current you" doesn't have to worry about a thing because that coworker who's always rude to you took a job somewhere else, you now own your own extremely successful business, and the friend who used to constantly complain feels fantastic and has nothing to say but positive things!

You're able to live in the moment (which isn't so bad) without thinking about the past or future, because everything totally works out. Your "future self" is loving life, and that is what you have to look forward to. All you need to do is be here now. The future will take care of itself, and the past is old news.

3. E-MOTION IS ENERGY IN MOTION

When energy moves through us, it takes the form of an emotion. When negative energy is trying to move through us, it takes the form of negative emotion.

Therefore, if you've been exposed to lots of negative energy, your body and mind are going to try to release it as such. This is why an adjustment of your attitude may be in order.

Crying is an action that comes from inside and cleanses the emotions. Some people may see crying as a bad thing, making one even sadder. The truth is that we feel much better after a good cry. It elevates your vibration by making room for joy to come in. So play some sad songs and let it all out!

Take responsibility for your mood and choose not to stay in it. Realize that just as this energy moved into you, it must move out. Try not to be around others when in a bad mood so as not to spread the misery. Accept what it is, let it go, and allow yourself to move forward. The moment you start feeling a little depressed or begin having more and more negative thoughts, do not shrug it off and let it get worse. It's a slippery slope. The longer you ignore these emotions, the harder it will be to detach from them and live a happy, emotionally healthy life. Nip them in the bud!

If your life is balanced and you regularly set aside time to have fun and do things that make you feel happy,

Then no matter what life and other people throw at you, emotions won't affect you in such a negative way.

Everything will be much, much easier to handle, because your vibration will be naturally higher, and you won't easily attach to the negative energy of others.

However, if you wake up one day in a bad mood for "no apparent reason," you'll know that you have been neglecting that part of your life that brings you joy. So browse through your Happiness Catalog, make a "note to self," and know that this too shall pass.

 **LET'S TAKE ACTION! WORKSHEET:**

Create Your Happiness Catalog!

Happiness can only come from the experience of joy. No one can do it for you.

Write down at least 10 things that bring you joy. The next time you are feeling that your vibrational level has dipped and you need to adjust your attitude, revisit this happiness catalog to put balance back into your life by doing things that make you smile.

(Here are some examples if you need some help getting started: Playing your guitar, taking a bubble bath, going to the movies, taking your dog for a long walk, baking cookies, putting together a puzzle, dancing around the house to your favorite tunes, buying your favorite flowers at the market.)

HAPPINESS CATALOG:

1
2
3
4
5
6
7
8
9
10

Now Create Your "Note to Self"

Sit down and have your "future self" write a letter to your "current self." Use your imagination and fantasize! The sky's the limit! Tell your "current self" how amazing life is!

Dear Current Self,

_____

_____

_____

_____

_____

_____

_____

_____

_____

_____

_____

_____

_____

_____

_____

_____

_____

_____

_____

_____

Love,
Future Self

Life Script #44

Do You Know
Who Your
True *Friends* Are

Do You Know
Who Your True *Friends* Are
_____ . . . _____

Sometimes you have to find out who your real friends are the hard way. It's an unpleasant experience to go through. It's a hurtful experience but one you'll be glad you had in the long run. Even if it saddens you at first to find out that someone you cared about (and who you thought cared about you) doesn't, it's important to understand that knowing for certain who your true friends are is an essential ingredient to your happiness now and in the future.

Are you wondering if someone you know might be a "false friend"? If so, ask yourself these three questions:

1. WHAT IS THE BASIS OF OUR RELATIONSHIP?

For a moment, step back and be an observer. Is your friendship with this person based on something rather shallow and ego-driven, like acquiring money or status, doing favors, or making connections? Is the relationship based primarily on external benefits and physical gains or emotional fulfillment? Does it have a purpose in the material world or the spiritual world? Is it a professional acquaintance or a personal attachment?

In theory, it's great to be able to offer opportunities to others to "get ahead," but then ask yourself, "Could the friendship survive if the money, favors, and other perks of advancement were to go away?" The answer may be "no."

If the relationship is a heartfelt, meaningful one built on a solid foundation, then the fleeting, superficial stuff won't matter. True friendship is based on love, respect, and appreciation for one another, which can never be bought or negotiated.

349

2. IS THERE AN EVEN EXCHANGE OF ENERGY BETWEEN US?

A friendship should be a 50/50 give and take. If you feel like you're giving a lot more than the other person, be it emotionally, financially, or in any other way, the relationship will not last.

Innocently, you may be coming from a place of love and harmony, not realizing that the other person only knows how to experience fear and separation. It's very possible that you've befriended a narcissist: an individual who is overly self-involved and addicted to their own wants, needs, and sense of importance.

These folks glean satisfaction only through the attention and admiration of others. The minute you stop trying to please them, they cut ties with you, which ironically, happens to be the greatest gift they could give you. Unfortunately, because of their alienating behavior, they end up losing all who've tried to placate and enable them, everyone who fed their ego addiction.

In essence, a person of this nature holds the perception that they are right and everyone else is wrong because they aren't able to see themselves as the common denominator. They blame other people and circumstances for their lot in life and believe the world is happening to them.

Becoming friends with someone intending to give without receiving, or receiving from them without giving, creates an uneven dynamic from the get-go.

All one-sided relationships are doomed to fail because the energy has to balance itself out one way or another.

One person cannot be the taker and "energy drainer" while the other is the giver and "energy drainee." True friends do for each other. True friends are equals. One doesn't drain the other for all they're worth.

When dependency of one person upon another develops, that is an unhealthy situation. A person can't be needy while simultaneously oblivious to the needs of others. It just doesn't work that way.

The Universe won't support it.

Have you long sacrificed your own needs for a "friend's," yet they expect you to keep right on making those sacrifices for them indefinitely—no matter what? That's a very conditional type of arrangement.

The reality is that their load isn't one you should have to carry, and they should have the common sense and decency to know that. In a true friendship, the individual who's been doing less than their fair share must eventually show that they care enough about you to take care of their own needs, let alone give back a little. Balance has to occur between two people or the relationship will implode.

3. DOES IT FEEL DISHONEST OR OBLIGATORY?

Your intuition is your greatest tool of knowing. Do you have a "friend" who is nice to you, but you kind of get the feeling that they're only nice because they think they have to be? Is it truly a friendship or is it a matter of them doing what they feel they have to do to get what they want?

Maybe they're nice just because they don't believe they have a choice. Maybe they feel obligated to be nice to you because you're their boss. Or perhaps you simply have something they want and they don't have enough confidence in themselves and their abilities to obtain it on their own.

Be discerning. Appearances can be deceiving. Insincere people can be charming and seemingly genuine, but when you no longer have what they want, they don't need to be nice to you anymore, and you find out pretty quickly who they are and how they honestly feel about you.

Don't take it too hard if you've experienced one of these scenarios, or are still experiencing it. You're not alone. Acquaintances come and go, but true friends are for life. There is no time or space, so you can always start over and move on. Lesson learned.

*When all is said and done,
The best friend you'll ever have should be you.*

Love yourself, and you'll naturally attract the right people into your life who love you, too.

LET'S TAKE ACTION! WORKSHEET:

Time to Examine Your Friendships

Are you wondering if someone you know might be a "false friend"? If so, ask yourself these questions to help figure it out:

1) For a moment, step back and be an observer. Is your friendship with this person based on something rather shallow and ego-driven, like acquiring money or status, doing favors, or making connections? Is the relationship based primarily on external benefits and physical gains or emotional fulfillment? Does it have a purpose in the material world or the spiritual world? Is it a professional acquaintance or a personal attachment? In theory, it's great to be able to offer opportunities to others to "get ahead," but then ask yourself, "Could the friendship survive if the money, favors, and other perks of advancement were to go away?"

_____

_____

_____

_____

2) Is the friendship a 50/50 give and take?

_____

_____

3) Do you have a "friend" who is nice to you, but you kind of get the feeling that they're only nice because they think they have to be? Is it truly a friendship or is it a matter of them doing what they feel they have to do to get what they want?

_____

_____

_____

"Let yourself be silently drawn by the
strange pull of what
you really love.
It will not lead you astray."

- Rumi

CHAPTER 9

Accepting the
Guidance
Around You

Life Script #45

Today's Lesson

Today's

———— . . . ————

Today, like every other day, is more than likely going to present you with an opportunity to expand your consciousness. You probably will not recognize it immediately as it is happening. For instance, you receive a phone call that delays you or even ruins your plans for the day altogether, or you unexpectedly encounter a stranger who could use some help, or maybe your feelings get terribly hurt by someone close to you.

Whatever the situation, the question should always be the same:

"*What am I being taught today?*

Patience? Surrender? Forgiveness? Gratitude? Self-Worth? Humility? Compassion?"

You will undoubtedly find that underlying themes show up in your life in many different forms. Understanding this principle allows you to be centered in the midst of perceived chaos.

So, will you learn what's being taught in today's lesson, or will you have to repeat it? The key to this understanding is to take a step back and recognize the purpose of the scenario that is occurring right in front of you. Awareness is ninety percent of getting beyond it.

The situation will have you feeling a certain way.

Let this energy pass through you instead of storing it deep down inside to deal with at some later time,

because each time you experience it, more of that energy will be needing to be released, so releasing it will only get harder. And you'll feel it because that sort of tamped-down energy will throw you off-balance, literally.

Every time a lesson is presented, it offers a chance to get rid of negative energy that has been pushed down and internalized. The Universe will send signals to you to get your attention. Small at first, then increasing in intensity. So the question is, will you heed the "Caution Up Ahead" sign, the "Detour 1000 ft." sign, or will you wait til you see the "BRIDGE OUT!" sign?...The sooner you learn the lesson, the better.

If you choose to learn what your consciousness is teaching you (because it is a choice) and you don't want to feel like you're Bill Murray in the movie Groundhog Day, then take note of these three ways to gain awareness and remain cool, calm, and centered no matter what happens:

1. BE THE AUDIENCE

Our lives are like soap operas. Hopefully, they're not that melodramatic, but much of the time it feels that way. From day to day, we have little or no idea what the heck is going to transpire. We simply try to cope with things as they come.

But I can't emphasize strongly enough the importance of not getting pulled in.

By that, I mean you should not be giving your power away to anything or anyone. The moment you do, the situation has just gained control of your emotions. You are no longer the master of your own life; you are a pawn.

Realize that situations are brought to you and dumped in your lap for a reason. Nothing is random. Therefore, instead of jumping right in headfirst without looking—observe. Watch the situation unfold. Who are the players? What are they doing? Have they done this before? Probably.

Where do you fit into all of this? Do you need to be a part of it? Is this really about being patient or accepting or possibly something else? What could happen differently this time so that today is the last time this scenario is brought to you?

Be an audience member during a performance of the latest show, not one of the actors, and you will be amazed at how much less dramatic your life becomes.

2. FEEL THE FEELING

We've all been embarrassed at some point or another or felt left out or that we weren't important enough or loved.

Scenarios that bring up these types of feelings are typically commentaries on our self-worth.

Whatever the underlying theme, we have built up a resistance in an effort to avoid the pain. That wall we use to protect ourselves gets higher and wider every time we get hurt. The only way to break down our walls is to recognize that these unpleasant feelings bring to our attention limitations we have placed upon ourselves: "I'm not good enough," "I don't deserve to be loved," "I'm stupid."

When you become aware of what's going on, relax and smile.

Take hold of your personal power and do not give it away.

You are the master of your thoughts and emotions; they are a choice. You choose them. Don't allow someone else to do it. When you remain in control and don't fall victim to the same scenario, these hurtful moments will be history.

3. SEE THE GIFT

Gifts are not always fun to receive, nor are they always wrapped up in neat little packages. They can be messy and uncomfortable. But the messy kind are the greatest gifts because they are life-changers. They may look like nothing you could ever want at the time, yet I guarantee you, the amount of positive energy and blessings that those gifts have the power to bring into our lives is boundless. We just need to accept them graciously and say, "Thank you." Recognize that gifts come in all shapes and sizes, but you have to be willing to see their true form. Everything is a gift.

Don't go through life blindly, living the same day over and over and over again. It's sad that so many people do this until they drive straight off a cliff! Be open to the lesson presented at that moment and move on. Your life will be so much happier, easier, and fuller because of it.

LET'S TAKE ACTION! WORKSHEET:

How to Center Amidst Chaos

Situations are brought to you and dumped in your lap for a reason. Next time chaos ensues, come back to this page to analyze the situation and learn its lesson so you can be centered in the middle of perceived chaos:

Who are the players? What are they doing? Have they done this before? Where do you fit into all of this? Do you need to be a part of it? Is this really about being patient or accepting, or possibly something else? What am I being taught today? Patience? Surrender? Forgiveness? Gratitude? Self-Worth? Humility? Compassion? Now write down what could happen differently so that this scenario is never again brought to you.

Life
Script
#46

Pay Attention to
the Messages

Pay Attention to the
Messages

We're all receiving many messages from various sources these days. Some are telling us the world is progressing forward, while others are convinced that it's heading backward. Of course, the news that is of the most value is what resonates in our hearts as we try to keep our egos out of the way, which is not easy.

Remember, the ego walks a fine line and can disguise itself to look like our "feelings." And even though particular views and beliefs may be what we stand for in our hearts, are we taking the messages we hear too far?

Have we convinced ourselves that our information is the only information and that it's our job to force that "information" on other people?

If we have to be right, then haven't our egos taken over?

It's of the utmost importance at this point in history that we put some space between ourselves and the chaotic, opposing energies surrounding us daily. There are always two sides to every story, and the truth undoubtedly lies somewhere in between. Look deeper and pay attention. Messages of truths AND messages of untruths are all around. Open your eyes and ears to these three ways of deciphering the messages you're receiving:

1. QUESTION EVERYTHING

Dig. Do your research. Never accept a situation or person at face value. All may not be as it seems. Is there more to the story than what you are being told? Do you believe everything you hear? Do you need to follow someone else, or can you make up your own mind? Are they revealing the truth, or are they masters at concealing it? Do the people you place all of your trust in have ulterior motives behind the scenes? Are you following a person based on blind faith and outer appearances, or do you have all the facts? Each of us must decide for ourselves.

2. PRETEND CARING

The unawakened ego needs to prove to others how caring and unselfish it is. Ask yourself what the motivation or incentive is for someone who is all about caring. Could they be promoting themselves as caring based on some goal other than wanting to help another?

Be it a corporation trying to sell you a product or a politician trying to gain your allegiance, the true goals may be financial and/or power-driven. Maybe there is something more useful to them (not you) going on in the background. Who and what is it that they really care about? Are they standing up for a cause by sending love and peace to support it, or are they mainly sending anger and hate against its opposition?

One cannot promote love while striking out in anger or being led by greed.

Neither loud, angry people nor people who are quietly in service to themselves create a peaceful, caring world.

3. CONTROL THROUGH FEAR

Seeing anything or anyone as 100% good or 100% bad is placing a judgment and label on that which is based in separation and individual perception. Every person is at a different level of awareness, so our perceptions are highly individualistic.

For instance, an individual who is "less aware" is more apt to be fearful, which only perpetuates their belief in the fear by adding energy to it. Whenever one feels fear, it is a sign that the person has given their power away.

They are unable to recognize that fear is a means of control by others.

When they're afraid, they allow other people and events to control them through confusion and division.

The truth of the matter is,
no person and no thing has more control
over your life than you do,
so you have nothing to fear.

Your power lies in the light that you hold inside, which you bring to the world. But if you forget that you indeed have that infinite power, then you fall prey to fear and the belief in some other human being or leader or corporation or whatever to "save" you.

Unplug from the television and your smartphone for a moment and look within for the answers. They are there. Trust your intuition, the messages of your heart. You will not find truth anywhere else.

LET'S TAKE ACTION! WORKSHEET:

Practice Questioning Everything...

Particular views and beliefs may be what we stand for in our hearts, but are we taking the messages we hear too far? Think of a particular belief or view you hold onto very strongly and let's play "devil's advocate" by answering the below questions:

Have you ever really questioned this view and its origin? Where did it come from? Does someone stand to gain anything by you having this belief? Could this belief or view come from fear? Could the true goals be financial and/or power-driven? Who and what is it that they really care about? Are they sending love and peace to support a cause, or are they mainly sending anger and hate against its opposition?

Life Script #47

Life Is How You See It

How You See It

— • • —

Life is all about perception. What one person sees as reality may be completely different from what another person in the same situation may see. It all depends on how our individual thoughts, feelings, and behaviors shape our world.

If we could only take a moment and look—I mean really look—at how we react to situations and interact with other people, we would learn so much about ourselves. It is in this self-awareness that we ultimately find happiness. We'll call it "living life in the big picture."

There are three overall stances we can take in any life experience, and each one has the potential to show us a whole lot about our perceptions:

1. BUMPING HEADS

When people ruffle our feathers, it's because we allow ourselves to become negatively enmeshed in what's happening. For instance, maybe your child comes home from school in a bad mood. He or she apparently got their feelings hurt by another child and has decided to take it out on you. Your child has a complete meltdown right in front of you.

What do you do? Well, you start having a meltdown of your own right back at them, of course! The energy level quickly escalates as you allow your child to take you down the rabbit hole. And we all know that the only thing this accomplishes is major aggravation and frustration. No one is listening. Nothing is being learned. The rational parent in you has "left the building."

So, what is this situation supposed to show you in the grand scheme of things? It's probably pointing out that one or more of your beliefs is being challenged. It is true that your child's release of negative energy toward you technically had nothing to do with you. However, the fact that you became so worked up and knocked off-balance because of it does have something to do with you.

Step away and look at it from an observer's point of view. Are you seeing in your child a side of yourself that you don't like? Is your child mirroring behaviors that you exhibit from time to time? Has he or she triggered feelings inside of you that need healing, like impatience, anger, or hurt?

This experience then becomes a positive one if you are able to learn from it. It gets you one step closer to your authentic self.

Think about it. It will help you understand and react more calmly to this type of unpleasant situation in the future.

2. SHUTTING DOWN

Shutting down is the other end of the spectrum. It means we have totally disengaged. This stance is equally ineffective. You avoid a situation altogether, and by doing so, you can never learn anything about it or yourself.

No evolving is allowed to occur.

Having interactions with others, no matter how difficult, is the way we find out who we are. There is intrinsic value in going outside of our comfort zones. We grow as a result of it. I believe that is why each of us is here, to become who we truly are. And we'll never find that out unless we engage in the world around us, even though it can be painful. In the end, the rewards are quite worth it!

3. HOLDING SPACE

What do I mean by "holding space?" I mean staying centered, remaining balanced, and being present while not participating in the drama unfolding in front of you.

Picture yourself encased in a protective bubble. This bubble has a turquoise and pink iridescence to it. It represents your throat chakra (self-expression) and your heart chakra (feelings). From inside the bubble, you are essentially playing the role of witness to that which you see and hear. You are not taking this personally. You realize the situation is not about you. There are larger forces at work here. You are simply watching a movie.

You say to yourself, "This child is very upset. He must be in the middle of a life lesson." Allow him to feel and release what he needs to.

Remember that people are at different psychological and emotional levels. Try to see from that perspective.

Others have to be allowed to release in order to rise to the next level. If you try to fix or control the situation, you keep them from evolving. So show only love. Stay in "the continuum"—not too engaged, not too disengaged. It's a balancing act.

Project positive energy and show compassion, and the episode will almost instantly be defused because of it.

You will have passed a test, bringing you closer to becoming more of your true self, and your son or daughter will have learned more from your powerful, gentle example than anything else could possibly teach them.

Life experiences are meant to align our personality with our soul and all that it is made of: harmony, peace, love, and compassion. When we look for a deeper reason for the events that present themselves in our lives, we consciously participate in our soul's evolution.

If what someone does or says irritates you, upsets you, or otherwise "hits a nerve" in some way, it has to do with how you see yourself and the world around you. Let go of the need to control or dominate the situation. If you don't assume a defensive or critical stance and focus instead on the soul of the other person, you will move past the incident without allowing it to negatively impact you. You will have passed the test.

When you are able to see the bigger picture and realize what is genuinely going on, you will quietly and calmly become the master of your own life.

Your thoughts, feelings, and behaviors will carefully calibrate themselves with clarity, peace, understanding, and truth on the road to living a happy life. You will not need to prove your mastery. You will be living it. You will radiate your empowerment. It will come through in everything you say and do, and be deeply felt by others.

LET'S TAKE ACTION! WORKSHEET:

Change the Way You See Things

Think back to a time when you were upset about a situation - did you get pulled into the negativity? Why or why not? How could you have remained centered and balanced? Describe what a different, more positive outcome could have been. How could you have felt more empowered and peaceful in this situation by projecting positive energy and compassion?

Life Script #48

How to Unlock
The Magic of
Synchronicity

How to Unlock The Magic of
Synchronicity

Synchronicity is the coming together of events in such a way as to appear purely coincidental. These happenings are unexpected, improbable, and when viewed from a larger perspective, prove to be integral pieces that fit perfectly into one's life puzzle.

When you experience synchronistic events, it is confirmation that you are on the right path and that you're open to the potential of anything occurring in your life.

This energy that is defined by some as random, lucky, out-of-the-blue, or even miraculous can be created intentionally. The question is, "How?" The answer is, "When your desire surpasses your limiting beliefs."

You will be able to harness the power of synchronicity when your wish and expectation for an experience, conscious or subconscious, outweighs your limited thinking, fear, and uncertainty about it. At that point, things become much easier and start falling into place.

Anything you expect with confidence becomes a self-fulfilling prophecy.

Believing is seeing, not the other way around.

Here are three ways you can open the floodgates of synchronicity and allow your life to naturally flow in the best direction for you:

1. MOVE FORWARD AND BE SURPRISED

Always be open to all of life's possibilities and every experience that awaits you outside the box of logic. Let go of the where, when, why, and how. You've heard this before, but this is no joke: Surrender to the infinite Universe.

Never assume that you know what your path is or how it will be shown to you. Situations can change in an instant. You have to be willing to go with the flow. Just know that things can and will occur in your life unexpectedly. Be excited about all the abundance the Universe has lined up with your name on it!

Something that you may have dreamed of doing or having can be dropped into your lap from somewhere completely outside of your imagination, so never place limits on how something might materialize in your reality.

2. TAKE THE PATH OF LEAST RESISTANCE

Your external reality is a reflection of your internal reality. When who we truly are on the inside is in alignment with who we are on the outside, the path of least resistance comes into play.

We usually think of attracting or pulling in scenarios for ourselves, but instead, think of them as energetically falling down to us. Think gravity. There is a soup of potentials available to you based on your chosen alignment or beliefs. However, there must also be action on your part. It is essential to leave the house and go places where you can interact with these potentials of synchronicity.

You've got to get up, go, and place yourself within the system. The scenario that is most likely follows the path of least resistance and shows up in your life.

3. TRUST AND FOLLOW YOUR FIRST INSTINCT

Synchronicity is a heart-soul connection process. Your heart's guidance is the force that will ultimately manifest that which is for your highest good.

Listen to your feelings about certain people, places, and things. Your intuition about them is your soul communicating with you. It will never steer you wrong. If particular places or groups of people make you feel joyful or passionate about life, then put your energies toward those things.

Joy is your GPS,
and synchronicity provides
the stops along the way!

Understand that the ease and flow of synchronicity is a system of energy in which we can choose to engage. This system is all around us waiting to facilitate our needs, but if we never open the door, nothing is ever going to happen.

Synchronicity is the energy that aligns with purpose. Situations may look like random accidents, but they are not. Synchronicity comes piece by piece, and the key to receiving is to be actively involved in the process by putting energy in the direction you want to go. So, by all means, welcome new situations into your life with excitement and an open mind. Approach life with a sense of wonder and prepare to be amazed at what makes its way to you.

LET'S TAKE ACTION! WORKSHEET:

Create Your Synchronicity Miracles

Write down a list of situations you desire in your life:

What limiting beliefs or excuses could be preventing you from achieving these desires?

What are some positive actions you can take to erase those limiting beliefs or excuses?

What places, people or activities make you feel joyful?

How can you actively get involved with the above joyful things?

Next, get out your planner and schedule these things into your calendar for this month. Then do the same for the month after, and so on!

Life
Script
℞ #49

This One Law Will
Change Your Life

This One Law Will
Change Your Life
— • • • —

There are several Universal Laws, and I'm sure you've heard of some, like the Law of Attraction and the Law of Cause and Effect.

But have you heard of the Law of Correspondence?

It's possible that you haven't, and it may be the most important one of all.

As you've guessed, it has to do with correspondence or communication. But it isn't about our communication with one another. It speaks to how we communicate with different parts of ourselves.

Most information you will read about the Law of Correspondence addresses the unique relationship between the Inner Self and the Outer Self, one being a reflection of the other. I'd like to take it one step further and suggest that there is a third essential component to consider when understanding how this law works, and that is the relationship with the Higher Self.

No doubt you're aware of the expressions, "As above, so below," and "On earth, as it is in heaven." Well, these ideas pertain to the line of communication, or correspondence, between the lower energies of the physical mind (earth) and the higher energies of the Divine Mind (heaven).

The key to changing your physical reality is by realizing that you are more of a spiritual being than a physical one. Every step you take in your physical life reflects the spiritual self that is trying to be realized, which is why lessons are repeated in our lives over and over again until we learn them.

When the transference of energy from our minds in the form of thoughts, emotions, actions, and words does not reflect a Higher Wisdom, this lower vibrational energy is, in essence, rejected and returned to us to revisit the same frequency until there is a match.

This is why you can be overwhelmed with an emotion or situation you are dealing with. Instead of calling upon your Higher Self to assist in a resolution, your lower energies are being sent out and returned to you, saying, "Try again." This is a constant motion that occurs in each situation of our lives.

The Law of Correspondence teaches us to acknowledge and examine an issue until it is healed.

When one's ability to move through a challenge gets closer and closer to being aligned with Divine Wisdom (by coming from a perspective of peace and love), then those negative, difficult types of situations will stop recurring in one's reality. This is when profound change can occur.

So how does understanding the Law of Correspondence shift our perception of the events that happen on the physical level? And how do we stay emotionally stable and wise amid the chaos? Let's investigate three ways in which we can make a conscious effort to align with the Higher Self and receive its guidance at times when the lower, physical self is presented with unpleasant circumstances:

1. THE MIRROR IMAGE

When you find yourself having a negative experience, recognize that somewhere there is disharmony in your inner world, and your outer world is reflecting that back to you. In other words, your Mirror Image is not of the True Self; it is of the damaged self.

You are being shown the changes that need to be made and the places in your subconscious that need to be healed.

When a negative emotion is triggered, it is important to take the time to understand why you're feeling a particular way and how you're reacting to it. Are you relating to your Higher Self or your physical self?

This is an important consideration, because when you access your Divine Mind, the higher part of your existence, then you allow that mirror of your I Am Presence, which is Who You Truly Are, to be revealed within your physical body.

When you take time to change the negative inner thoughts and feelings into positive affirmations, that's when you are aligning with your Inner Truth. It is a moment in time in which you allow the true Spirit of You to become the Physical You.

2. THE OPPOSING FORCE

*Once you discover the lower frequencies
happening in your outer world,
you can transform them to a higher
frequency by applying opposite energy.*

Since our energy is reflected back to us at all times, know that when you are faced with something negative, the quickest way to dissipate that energy, heal your subconscious, and connect to your Higher Self is to react in an opposite fashion.

When you are criticized, praise someone.

When you are hurt, love someone.

When you are discouraged, encourage someone.

When you are afraid, reassure someone.

At that moment, you are mastering the ability to heal a wounded part of you. You react from your soul's perspective, and thus, you recognize that we are One.

*When you feed the energy that you desire,
focusing on good and positive thoughts,
the opportunity for healing is created.*

3. THE FLOW OF LIFE

Imagine yourself floating on a raft along a lazy river, completely letting go and trusting in your safety. Each moment flows beautifully into the next. You have no doubt, not one thought that anything is not as it should be.

To live your life in peace and serenity is to live in harmony with the law of correspondence. However, when you encounter rough seas and find yourself being tossed about, that's the wake-up call that your rocky outer world requires some fine-tuning by your inner world.

The only lasting change that can take place is from within.

Only then will it show up on the outside. Real change comes from the Higher Mind (as above) into the Lower Mind (so below). Many think that changing the outside temporarily will result in a new, happier life, but they find out, eventually, that the only permanent change comes from the inside, which should always accept guidance from the Higher Self.

Try to flow with life as it happens, and when you feel a jolt, stop and ask yourself where the line of communication between your Divine Self and your Physical Self has broken down. More than likely, you will immediately see the discrepancy, which will make you better prepared and aligned next time.

It has become more and more important for each of us to be responsible for our personal evolution and growth so that the world can be heaven on earth. But until that time, the fundamental challenge is being honest with yourself and realizing the potential you hold to create change on the inside and all around.

LET'S TAKE ACTION! WORKSHEET:

Using Opposing Forces

When you are faced with something negative, the quickest way to dissipate that energy, heal your subconscious, and connect to your Higher Self is to react in an opposite fashion. Using the Law of Correspondence, let's transform lower frequencies to a higher frequency by applying opposite energy.

Think of a past or future scenario for each of the below prompts and then practice applying the opposite energy to that situation!

1 EXPLAIN A SCENARIO IN WHICH YOU WERE <u>CRITICIZED</u>:

What will you do to praise someone in this situation?

Apply the opposite energy →

2 EXPLAIN A SCENARIO IN WHICH YOU WERE <u>HURT</u>:

What will you do to love someone in this situation?

Apply the opposite energy →

3 EXPLAIN A SCENARIO IN WHICH YOU WERE <u>DISCOURAGED</u>:

What will you do to encourage someone in this situation?

Apply the opposite energy →

4 EXPLAIN A SCENARIO IN WHICH YOU WERE <u>AFRAID</u>:

What will you do to reassure someone in this situation?

Apply the opposite energy →

Life Script #50

The *Energy* Around Us

The *Energy* Around Us

We've all noticed how the energy of an entire room can change whenever certain people enter it. Phil lifts up your spirit with his upbeat attitude and makes you feel good all day. Carol, on the other hand, makes you feel like running for the emergency exit!

Every one of us brings energy to our coworkers, loved ones, and even the stranger in line behind us at the grocery store. It would serve us well to realize that

> *The energy we radiate affects others' lives and that we need to be responsible for it.*

The following are three ways that we can recognize what we're "putting out there," how to deal with people who don't, and why it's so important:

1. VIBRATE RESPONSIBLY

Ask yourself this question: "Are you taking responsibility for the energy you're bringing to others?" If you've had a tough day, do you make sure everybody hears about it? Does everyone know how unfairly you think things have played out in your life? Do you have "pity parties" for yourself on a regular basis? (You know who you are.) When you come home from work, school, or wherever, does your family immediately sense whether you've had a good day or a bad one? Believe me, they do. They can feel your energy.

We live on a vibrational planet. Everything on the planet vibrates, including people. We are either emanating a high vibration or a low vibration. A high vibration results from feelings of happiness, love, respect, and so forth. A low vibration comes from the emotions of anger, depression, stress, and so on.

When you come home to your family or go to work each day, recognize how your vibration affects and influences the degree of joy or sadness in other people's lives. Step back and check yourself. What type of energy are you carrying from place to place and person to person? Is it going to enhance someone else's well-being or deplete it?

If you're embracing a positive, high vibration, and you encounter someone who is radiating a negative, low vibration, you have two choices. You can maintain your alignment with that positive vibration by politely excusing yourself from them or staying and deciding not to attach to their petty dramas. The other option is to lower yourself to the other person's negative vibration and let their drama change your mood for the worse.

For those times when you encounter particular individuals who, without fail, "push your buttons" no matter how hard you try to remain centered, remember that when you start getting all worked up, those people are your "Peace Teachers." They are teaching you how to find peace. They are testing you! You can pass the test by learning to be peaceful as an alternative to anger or frustration, accepting that they are who they are, and it is what it is.

2. JOIN THE CLUB!

Have you ever noticed how certain people gravitate toward each other? In school, we called them "cliques." For instance, if you look closely enough, you'll tend to see that people who are always complaining about something seem to be friends with other complainers. Those who are rather judgmental usually hang out with people who also hold critical views. And consequently, folks who like to laugh and just have fun normally get together with others who have similar interests and a shared sense of humor.

To put it another way, animal rights organizations don't attract members that enjoy hunting, and hunting clubs don't attract vegetarians. On the other hand, angry people do attract other angry people, and happy people do attract other happy people.

Individuals who are on the same vibrational level are magnets to one another.

Therefore, be the type of person you would like to attract to yourself. Be the kind of person you'd like to have as a friend. Take a moment and look around you. What "clubs" have you joined?

3. THE RIPPLE EFFECT

Let's look at "the big picture." When we contribute to a shift in another person's energy, either positively or negatively, it affects humanity on a much larger scale. It's like throwing a rock into a lake and watching the ripples of water multiply and get bigger, traveling farther and farther out until they spread so far and wide that the ripples eventually become one with the body of water as a whole.

When you "throw out" that one smile or helping hand to someone who needs it, you spark a "ripple effect." Creating change in a person's energy toward the positive raises their vibration. In turn, they will then affect whomever they come into contact with, and on and on and on.

Conversely, that one rude comment or little "meltdown" can spark the ripple effect in a negative way. Who knows how many people could end up shifting into a lower vibration because of something you said or did without even thinking about the consequences? Everything we say and do does matter. We have a lot more power than most of us realize.

Let's choose to be more self-aware and really stop and think about our words, our actions, and our attitudes before we combine our energies with the energies of others. Are we communicating truths that are meaningful and necessary? Do our words and behaviors build people up or tear them down? Let's be thoughtful and considerate when it comes to the lives of those around us and bring the positive energy to each other that we all truly deserve.

LET'S TAKE ACTION! WORKSHEET:

Taking Responsibility for your Energy...

When we contribute to a shift in another person's energy, either positively or negatively, it affects humanity on a much larger scale. It's like throwing a rock into a lake and watching the ripples of water multiply and get bigger. Let's choose to be more self-aware and really stop and think about our words, our actions, and our attitudes before we combine our energies with the energies of others.

Ask yourself these questions and reflect below:

If you've had a tough day, do you make sure everybody hears about it?

Are you taking responsibility for the energy you're bringing to others?

Are you communicating truths that are meaningful and necessary?

Do your words and behaviors build people up or tear them down?

"The way to get started is to quit talking and begin doing."

-Walt Disney

CHAPTER 10

How to *Create* a Better Life

Life
Script
📄 #51

Everywhere You Are Is *Sacred* Space

Everywhere You Are Is
Sacred Space

It is becoming more and more prevalent these days with those who are spiritually-minded to create a sacred space within their home. They use the corner of a room to place candles, stones, or simply some of their favorite things where they can sit in silent meditation. Many people carry that idea over into their workplace and display pictures of loved ones and objects that are meaningful to them on a small area of their desk in order to feel grounded when their job becomes stressful.

I have to wonder if sacred space is confined to a particular place that we go to feel centered and peaceful. Instead of us going to it, why can't it come to us? Maybe sacred space can follow us around! Wouldn't it be nice to feel centered no matter where we are?

It all comes down to being aware that we are surrounded by peace and love—all the time. We need to pay attention to the close connection between our soul and our body.

Take a look at the following techniques and see if you can create your own sacred space wherever you are:

1. THE BUBBLE

Envision yourself inside a beautiful bubble of light. This bubble can be iridescent, or white, or any color that you love. Practice being in the sanctity of this cocoon. Sit in it, walk around, do whatever you want to do, but remain in your imaginary pod.

Everything around you is happening as usual, but nothing can come inside the sacred space of your bubble—no one else's drama, no stress, because while you are inside, you know that nothing can touch you. Its energy transcends whatever you are doing. All is peace and love.

2. THE MAGNET

As you go about your day, think of yourself as a human magnet. The only situations and individuals that are attracted to you (and vice versa) are positive and uplifting. Everything else simply falls away. The things that you want to have around you are made of metal. These wonderful people, places, and things that make you happy are drawn to you and stick like glue. All of the other stuff is just plastic.

3. THE MOVIE

Observe life as if you're watching a movie. Which people constitute the main cast of characters? Who are in the supporting roles? Stand back and look around. Is everyone acting their usual part? Are the same little episodes playing out just as they have a thousand times before?

Be an audience member. Does any of what is going on involve you, or can you detach from the scene? Do you need to be a part of the action, or is observing from an emotional distance a viable alternative? Make a cameo appearance when it's your cue. Otherwise, just keep watching.

4. THE SOUND OF MUSIC

Yes, this is, in fact, a movie, but I'm not suggesting that you start watching it every day. No, what I'm getting at here is the power of music to calm the mind and soothe the body. Investing in a pair of earbuds (or earplugs!) can be exactly what you need to create your portable sacred space.

Listening to relaxing music, or even enjoying total silence and tuning out the rest of the world for a short while, might be just what your psyche ordered. So when feasible, make quiet time for yourself anywhere you can. Let go of all the unnecessary noise around you. Getting some real peace and quiet, even for a brief moment in the day, is extremely helpful in centering the Self.

5. THE WALK

We all walk from here to there during the course of a busy day. Make that time count as sacred time. Be mindful of your body's movement. Feel your arms and legs cutting through the thickness of the air. Ideally, find a way to walk outside as much as possible, even if it's through the middle of a bustling city. Experts say the fresh air does wonders for a person, and they're right.

When away from city life, being surrounded by trees, water, rocks, birds, and grass is healing in every way.

Let nature speak to you.
Listen to it.
Become a part of it.

Be open to its ancient teachings of growth, death, and rebirth —the cycle of life.

Walking on a tree-lined trail can feel like an outdoor cathedral that fills you with reverence and awe. Your cares and concerns will seem small. And when your cares and concerns are small, you have a golden opportunity to find real peace.

6. THE COMMUTE

Whether you are driving back and forth from the office, soccer practice, taking the train into town for the day, or flying for business or pleasure, while traveling you can regroup and make plans. During your travels exists useful, quiet time that should not be overlooked.

Traveling time that is spent alone can be "you time." Use those moments in the day to focus on your breathing, positive thoughts, and intentions. Don't think about work or what you have to do next. Be present in those minutes or hours. That time should be spent getting to know yourself, nurturing your connection with Spirit, and thinking of all the wonderful gifts for which you have to be grateful.

Make no mistake about it. You can take your sacred space with you. With practice, doing so will feel essential to your body's DNA. As each day passes, a sense of serenity will grow inside of you until it profoundly transforms your everyday existence. You will dwell in your personal sanctuary, and your personal sanctuary will dwell in you.

Connect to the energy of your soul by living in sacred space, and you'll find peace.

**LET'S TAKE ACTION!
WORKSHEET:**

Sacred Spaces Check-List

It's time to practice creating your sacred spaces! Go through the below techniques and see if you can create your own sacred space wherever you are! Check the box once you've completed each one:

☐ 1) **The Bubble:** Envision yourself inside a beautiful bubble of light. This bubble can be iridescent, or white, or any color that you love. Practice being in the sanctity of this cocoon. Sit in it, walk around, do whatever you want to do, but remain in your imaginary pod.

☐ 2) **The Movie:** Observe life as if you're watching a movie. Which people constitute the main cast of characters? Who are in the supporting roles? Stand back and look around. Is everyone acting their usual part? Are the same little episodes playing out just as they have a thousand times before?

_____

_____

_____

☐ 3) **The Magnet:** As you go about your day, think of yourself as a human magnet. The only situations and individuals that are attracted to you (and vice versa) are positive and uplifting.

☐ 4) **The Walk:** Next time you are on a walk, be mindful of your body's movement. Feel your arms and legs cutting through the thickness of the air. Ideally, find a way to walk outside as much as possible, even if it's through the middle of a bustling city.

☐ 5) **The Sound of Music:** Make quiet time for yourself anywhere you can. Let go of all the unnecessary noise around you. Getting some real peace and quiet, even for a brief moment in the day, is extremely helpful in centering the Self.

Life Script #52

Your Life is a Puzzle

Your Life is a

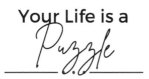

Consider for a moment that your life is a puzzle. It may be a simple puzzle with a hundred different pieces, or it may be a more complicated thousand-piece puzzle with a picture that's rather tricky to put together. Either way, as you work through this puzzle of life, you're more than likely going to try forcing some wrong pieces into the empty spaces. They look like they should fit, but as you continue on, it becomes clearer that they're just not meant to line up that way. So what should you do? Well, break it apart, of course, and reassemble those pieces the right way.

Now examine your life. Maybe you think things are moving along fairly smoothly. Your family looks happy. Your job seems to be progressing just fine. Then one day, you find out you've been released from your position at work and the boss you thought of as a friend, the one you relied upon to help further your career, has betrayed you. You're blindsided by this situation. Everything you thought was perfect completely collapses.

Or maybe your wedding is just around the corner—invitations sent, flowers ordered, family excited—and your fiancé calls it off. You beat yourself up about it thinking, "How could I have made such a terrible mistake?"

My answer to you is this:
Your puzzle was put together the wrong way.

But the wrong way is often the right track. It's wonderful to be "wrong" once in a while. It may hurt quite a bit, but it's always to your advantage when the truth is unveiled. Being shown that type of information is priceless.

Taking a close look at your life, you may realize that a few puzzle pieces need rearranging or perhaps an entire section needs to be taken apart. But whatever the size of the challenge, mistakes are gifts. The reason being wrong is so right is that

wrong allows change to come in, and change is the fuel that we burn to grow and evolve.

Never be afraid to trust someone, open your own business, or fall in love. You might just be "wonderfully wrong." And if you are, welcome the opportunity to break apart those pieces of your puzzle, change their position, and put them back in a new way. Because when you do, you'll realize that you're now one step closer to seeing the whole picture and having all of the pieces interlock at exactly the perfect points.

Build your life just as you would a puzzle, piece by piece, section by section.

You may get bored at times, or frustrated, or feel as though you'd rather give up. What you must do, however, is know that all of the pieces are there, and the more tenaciously you try to place them where they belong, the more connections you'll discover. Soon you will begin to visualize and discern images as they come together to form the overall vision of your life.

Do you have a vision? What does your puzzle look like? Is it falling into place, or are you forcing the pieces to fit where they don't belong? If it's the latter, reorganize, readjust, and reexamine what's in front of you. The answers are right there. And, at this very moment, a surprisingly stunning picture of your life is revealing itself—one piece at a time.

LET'S TAKE ACTION! WORKSHEET:

Your Puzzle...

Do you have a vision? What does your puzzle look like? Is it falling into place, or are you forcing the pieces to fit where they don't belong?

Life Script #53

Sting:

The Guy Who Has It All Figured Out

Sting:

The Guy Who Has It All Figured Out

———— • • • ————

A few years ago, I had the distinct privilege of meeting Sting. Many people think he's just about the coolest guy on the planet. Others are sure he's a prima donna (after all, he is a celebrity). Well, I'm here to tell you exactly who this guy is.

At The Public Theater in New York City (a unique historic venue for artists of all types), Sting had been performing his new CD titled The Last Ship, which also made its debut on Broadway as a musical. The premise of the work is based on the local shipbuilding industry in the town of Wallsend, England, where Sting lived as a boy.

After arriving at The Public, I and other patrons sat upstairs in the Levin Lounge waiting until it was time to say "hello" to Sting. By the way, all of the proceeds from the tickets purchased for the event were given to support The Public Theater and its endeavors.

As I sat in the lounge, two lovely young women who represented the theater and were integral in coordinating the performances came over to speak to me. They were both magnificent at their jobs, making sure everyone was completely comfortable.

Both had been around Sting for many days as the rehearsals and shows were underway, and told me of their enjoyable encounters with him. The ladies appeared extremely genuine and their comments truly heartfelt, but I was determined to find out for myself what vibe I would get from the star during our brief one-on-one, as well as throughout the concert.

To my excitement, we were promptly ushered into a small room an hour before the show. On the walls hung artwork created by one of his childhood friends depicting scenes of the ships he had watched being built.

Suddenly, Sting appeared in the room clad in a worn T-shirt and jeans with work boots on his feet. He had no sense of pretension whatsoever, smiling from ear to ear, as if the pleasure were all his. Charming and sporting an air of peaceful dignity, he looked decades younger than his chronological age and was interested in every person. My only thought:

" *Wow. This guy has got it all figured out.* "

As we were then shown to our seats for the show, I noticed his wife, Trudie Styler (also looking twenty years younger than her apparent age and stunning in person), with their children in tow, walking in to see her husband's performance. The love and admiration that his family held for him and his achievements was undeniable.

As Sting took the stage with several other musicians and singers, he explained how the entire project began. He said he took himself "out of the way" to honestly portray the harsh, yet passionate, day-to-day lives of the men who built the ships.

The emotions and songs simply flowed through him.

He told us that as a boy, the sheer behemoth scale of these ships was quite a sight to see. However, the work that those men did and the lives that they led were extremely hard. Sting knew from an early age that his purpose in life would lead him on a different path, and without a doubt, he was right.

Even expressing that new music from the point of view of the struggling shipbuilders, the lyrics and delivery were animated, fun, and engaging. The audience got a genuine glimpse of this downtrodden yet delightful and spirited group of people. In the intimate 260-seat Anspacher Theater inside The Public, all were stomping their feet and clapping their hands! I glanced back at Trudie, who was sitting on the edge of her seat, a notable amount of pride welling up inside of her.

Before, during, and after the show, I observed the interaction between Sting and his fellow performers on stage. His humility, graciousness, and obvious respect for the talent of these individuals were palpable. Their feelings toward him were more than mutual.

I was in awe of the positive energy radiating off of the stage

The bottom line is that Sting didn't have to give a voice to these stalwart men of maritime history and their families who withstood the trials and tribulations of their class, nor did he have to bring their story to a venue where the money paid to see his concert could be used to benefit the arts and the outreach programs that The Public Theater champions, nor did he have to meet with any of us.

Sting looks so good and so happy and is so successful because (aside from the fact that he oozes talent)

he lives from a place of joy.

He makes music that feeds his soul, is enthusiastic about promoting and supporting the work of gifted artists from all walks of life, feels honored and humbled in the presence of others, and allows himself to experience new joy in every moment, then shares it with the rest of the world.

My friends, Sting has it all figured out . . . and I'm quite certain he would humbly disagree.

LET'S TAKE ACTION! WORKSHEET:

Inspiration into Action

Who do you admire for "having it all"? What is it about their life that inspires you? What actions can you take to move from inspiration to reality?

_____

_____

_____

_____

_____

_____

_____

_____

_____

_____

_____

_____

_____

_____

_____

_____

_____

_____

Life
Script
Rx #54

Twenty-Five Thought-Provoking Quotes About

Peace

Twenty-Five Thought-Provoking
Quotes About *Peace*

——— . . . ———

These are twenty-five of my favorite quotes on the subject of peace. Some of them address peace in the context of inner peace, some in the context of world peace, and some that view inner peace and world peace as one and the same.

These quotes have been chosen from a diverse group of individuals sharing their thoughts from different vantage points: ethnically, politically, socially, religiously, and so forth. But, of course, there are many, many more thought-provoking assertions on the topic. Feel free to add any of your favorites to this list so that we can, together, send as much "peace energy" as humanly possible out into the world!

1) Darkness cannot drive out darkness; only light can do that. Hate cannot drive out hate; only love can do that.

—Martin Luther King Jr.

2) What can you do to promote world peace? Go home and love your family.

—Mother Teresa

3) Peace cannot be kept by force; it can only be achieved by understanding.

—Albert Einstein

4) We can never obtain peace in the outer world until we make peace with ourselves.

—Dalai Lama

5) Nobody can bring you peace but yourself

—Ralph Waldo Emerson

6) A mind at peace, a mind centered and not focused on harming others, is stronger than any physical force in the Universe.

—Wayne Dyer

7) Peace is not made at the council table or by treaties, but in the hearts of men.

—Herbert Hoover

8) When the power of love overcomes the love of power, the world will know peace.

—Jimi Hendrix

9) We cannot be both the world's leading champion of peace and the world's leading supplier of the weapons of war.

—Jimmy Carter

10) Peace is not absence of conflict; it is the ability to handle conflict by peaceful means.

—Ronald Reagan

11) The most valuable possession you can own is an open heart. The most powerful weapon you can be is an instrument of peace.

—Carlos Santana

12) The soldier above all others prays for peace, for it is the soldier who must suffer and bear the deepest wounds and scars of war.

—Douglas MacArthur

13) There was never a good war, or a bad peace.

—Benjamin Franklin

14) An eye for an eye only ends up making the whole world blind.

—Mahatma Gandhi

15) Peace comes from within. Do not seek it without.

—Buddha

16) One cannot reflect in streaming water. Only those who know internal peace can give it to others.

—Lao Tzu

17) Making peace is harder than making war.

—Adlai Stevenson

18) Courageous people do not fear forgiving, for the sake of peace.

—Nelson Mandela

19) If civilization is to survive, we must cultivate the science of human relationships—the ability of all peoples, of all kinds, to live together, in the same world at peace.

—Franklin D. Roosevelt

20) While you are proclaiming peace with your lips, be careful to have it even more fully in your heart.

—Francis of Assisi

21) A musician must make music, an artist must paint, a poet must write, if he is to be ultimately at peace with himself.

—Abraham Maslow

22) Our most important task is to transform our consciousness so that violence is no longer an option for us in our personal lives, that understanding that a world of peace is possible only if we relate to each other as peaceful beings, one individual at a time.

—Deepak Chopra

23) If in our daily life we can smile, if we can be peaceful and happy, not only we, but everyone will profit from it. This is the most basic kind of peace work.

—Thich Nhat Hanh

24) The quest for peace begins in the home, in the school and in the workplace.

—Silvia Cartwright

And finally . . .

25) Peace is a conscious choice.

—John Denver

Yes, it is. Thank you, John Denver
. . . wherever you are.

LET'S TAKE ACTION! WORKSHEET:

Quote Keeper

Go back through the quotes in this script and circle your favorites. Do you have some other quotes that inspire you? Write them below!

Keep this page on hand so you can continue to collect your favorite quotes anytime you come across one that moves you.

QUOTE KEEPER

"You can tell a lot about a person by
the way they handle three things:
a rainy day, lost luggage and
tangled Christmas tree lights."

- Maya Angelou

CHAPTER 11

Surviving &
Loving the
Holidays

Life
Script
#55

Digesting the
Thanksgiving
Sandwich

Digesting the *Thanksgiving* Sandwich:

Three Tips for Those Parenting Children and Parents During the Holidays

—— • • • ——

Are you a certified member of the "Sandwich Generation?" Have you been placed in the middle of "parenting" an aging mom and/or dad while raising your own small children? Well, for Thanksgiving, I was always elected to be the hostess of the feast, and we all know how stressful and unnerving that day can become! So, to keep calm and maintain one's sanity, there are three very important things you can do to bring peace to your Thanksgiving festivities (without anyone else's cooperation):

1. BE THE WATERFALL

Think of yourself as the top of a waterfall. You are the hostess of the family gathering and the one everyone is looking to for direction in setting the tone for the day. Are you going to cascade over your loved ones the feelings of being frantic and overwhelmed, or relaxed and comfortable?

If you are not calm and centered, the older folks will become cranky and the children will start acting out and misbehaving. Your attitude affects theirs. They will feel your energy spilling out over them. If it's negative energy, you're going to see a negative outcome. If it's positive energy, you're going to see a positive outcome. So slow down, take your time, and set a pace that allows you to enjoy the fact that one or both of your parents are still here and can spend time with you and your children, and vice versa. Next year may be a different story. Be thankful!

If you are constantly being bothered by your parents, children, and others, the best way to have a peaceful day is to stop caring. I'm not suggesting that you stop caring about the people themselves and their highest good, it means that you should stop caring and investing your time in the things that they do. If we focus too heavily on the things we aren't getting back from the people we care about, all of our attention will be on issues of lack.

Give to yourself by taking a break from caring about what other people do.

Giving becomes not a depletion, but a circulation of prosperous energy that, as we enrich others, continually enriches us.

In your head, try acting out Thanksgiving from prep to cooking to serving at least once in the days leading up to the big event. Envision your parents and children enjoying each other's company and everything going smoothly in the living room while you calmly and joyfully cook in the kitchen and set out the food in the dining room. Use as much detail as possible, and it will become a self-fulfilling prophecy.

2. STOP SEEKING APPROVAL

Everything does NOT have to be perfect! It is no one else's business to approve what we do and how we do it—including your parents. You are an adult with a household of your own. You are in charge! You are no longer a child. You are not your parents. You are your true self. You are free to make choices and decisions.

Seeking approval from others gets us into all kinds of trouble. We agree to do things we don't want to do out of the fear that someone may disapprove of us if we say, "No."

They more than likely will never approve of many of the things you do anyway. The joke is that they're too busy seeking approval from you! So don't give your "power" away to your parents or your children or anyone else, for that matter. Remember that you are always in the right place at the right time doing the right thing.

Don't think about the past. You can't change it. But you can change its effect on the present. We may be clinging to childhood beliefs or experiences that are no longer relevant to our lives or our destinies. We may have old wounds, but we are not prisoners of our pasts, slaves of our memories. We are free—at any time—to discard those belief systems and behavioral patterns that belong to another place and time.

3. TRUST IN YOURSELF

Reserve the issue of trust for your relationship with yourself. Use your relationships with other people to teach you about love, honesty, growth, integrity, and non-attachment. Trusting others is great in theory, but it's almost impossible to put into practice.

Why? Because most of the time we only trust people when they do exactly what we want them to do. When they act otherwise, we feel disappointed and think they can no longer be trusted. But true trust is not about relying on others to meet our expectations. Instead, true trust means learning to rely on ourselves, which will help us to accept others for who they are, not who we want them to be.

Recognize who you are within. First and foremost, be true to you above all others. If we treat ourselves with kindness and compassion, then we'll treat others that way too. It's all very simple, but very important.

During autumn, think of yourself as a leaf. Sometimes we're vibrant and colorful, sometimes we fall and hit the ground, but we always bloom and grow and start anew. So, be still and let the wind carry you in whatever direction it wants you to go, and you'll have great peace in your life.

**LET'S TAKE ACTION!
WORKSHEET:**

Thanksgiving Peace

How will you take action to bring peace to your Thanksgiving
festivities this year? How can you continue to implement these
same peace strategies throughout the rest of your year?

_____

_____

_____

_____

_____

_____

_____

_____

_____

_____

_____

_____

_____

_____

_____

_____

Life Script #56

Thanksgiving:
Is It Only One Day a Year?

Thanksgiving:
Is It Only One Day a Year?

———— • • • ————

Most of us focus on being thankful for all that we have on a Thursday in November over a turkey dinner. But what happens on the other 364 days? Well, we go about our routines and obligations, becoming once again conscious of our dissatisfactions and wants. What we fail to realize, though, is that in every second of every one of those other 364 days, each of us is making an energetic choice to either create or destroy the moments of our lives until the next Thanksgiving Day rolls around.

For the most part, we are completely unaware of this added responsibility. It is indeed a full-time job. However, every word we speak and every thought we think counts. There are no exceptions. No free passes are given to those living unconsciously of this fact. Not one of us is excused from pulling in a future we did not intend, a future that simply materialized as a result of our attitudes and moods waffling back and forth reacting to all of life's little dramas.

The good news is we have the opportunity to change each moment that we live for the better.

If we could pay close attention to how we face the circumstances of each day, and recognize that this act of mindfulness is a significant, profound tool just waiting to be utilized, then we can also recognize that our daily energy, whether thankful or not, is the determining factor of our future.

Once we fully understand that we choose our alignment and point of attraction in every instant, that all of our power to create or destroy lies in the present time, not the past or the future, we will consciously begin to notice our reactions to everyday occurrences. Then we can begin to shift them in positive and meaningful ways.

Here are three changes in perception that we can make starting today in order to take immediate advantage of this year-long power of "thanksgiving," and live happier, more abundant lives.

1. FROM "HAVE TO" TO "GET TO."

When we know we have to do something that we consider a burden, we become the biggest obstacle to our happiness. We dismiss the present moment, judge the task, then place our focus on waiting for something better to come along once we get through it.

What we don't realize at the time, however, is that no matter what we "have to do," if our attitude toward it is negative, we are providing the Universe with a vibration that it will then make a priority and act upon.

Instead, what we need to do is choose to perceive the situation as something that has value, regardless of what it is

We then change the burden to an experience, an opportunity to create positive energy right then and there. You are constantly radiating energy. Is it going to be energy that is destructive to your future, or energy that resonates with love and excitement? In seeing that all is special, and that you "get to" experience even the smallest things each day, the magnetic vibration of your appreciative attitude has the power to change the direction of your entire life going forward.

2. FROM "IT SHOULDN'T BE" TO "IT IS WHAT IT IS."

The key to staying centered and peaceful no matter what is happening around you is acceptance. When you shift from a standpoint of judging a situation, yourself, or others, to accepting that there is a reason behind everything, a bigger picture that you may not comprehend, then you bring harmony, synchronicity, and abundance into your life. You step into the universal flow of energy, which supports an honoring, loving, joyous point of view that charges the moment with powerful energy.

3. FROM "I NEED" TO "I HAVE."

When we see what is missing from our lives, we perpetuate it. If you consistently observe lack in your life, the insufficiencies will grow. There are two universal laws at work here in particular: the Law of Paradoxical Intent and the Law of Magnetism.

The Law of Paradoxical Intent takes effect when you desire one thing but you focus on your dissatisfaction in not having it

Therefore, altering your words and thoughts from those of dissatisfaction to those of appreciation will elevate your resonance making you receptive, not resistant, to your desire.

When you recognize all of the good you already have in your life, you activate the Law of Magnetism.

This law states that if you are thankful, the Universe will bring you more to be thankful for. Unfortunately, however, the opposite is also true.

Send "Thank You" out into the Universe as much as possible! Keeping a gratitude journal is an extremely helpful tool for transforming an attitude of lack into an attitude of gratitude. Every night before bed, write down whatever you were grateful for that day, big or small—a promotion, a parking space, or someone who smiled at you. Think of as many things as possible. When you're having a tough day, pull out your journal and read about all of the wonderful things you've had to be thankful for. Your mood will certainly change for the better.

When you focus on making the present a joyful and loving experience, you don't dwell on the past or worry about the future anymore. Honoring the present moment with value and appreciation allows everything else to take care of itself.

Our moment-to-moment decisions define us. They are what determine the course of our lives. We not only need to stay conscious of what we are experiencing, but we also need to value it. Finding the joy in the here and now is the gateway to future joy.

Don't play the waiting game that someday you'll be happy. With your present energy, choose now.

Intend to enjoy the present and be thankful for it. All experiences are opportunities to create positive energy. The energetic seed of all future happiness is planted in the here and now.

The following is a blessing my father always used to give at the dinner table, especially on Thanksgiving Day. Since this will be our first Thanksgiving without him, I feel it is appropriate to pass it along to all of you.

Thank you, Lord, for the blessings of another day

For health and strength, for food and shelter

*For all the good things we have
and all the good things we may share*

May each succeeding day unfold beauty, wisdom, and love.

Amen

Wherever we are in the calendar year when you're reading this, Happy Thanksgiving!

LET'S TAKE ACTION! WORKSHEET:

How To Give Thanks All Year

Although Thanksgiving is "technically" one day a year, we often fail to realize that in every second of every one of those other 364 days, each of us is making an energetic choice to either create or destroy the moments of our lives until the next Thanksgiving Day rolls around.

What are the three changes in perception you will commit to making today to take immediate advantage of this year-long power of "thanksgiving," and live a happier, more abundant life?

1) _____

_____

_____

_____

2) _____

_____

_____

3) _____

_____

_____

Life
Script
Rx #57

How to *Rekindle*
Your Holiday Spirit

How to *Rekindle* Your Holiday Spirit

— • • • —

During the holidays, do you often wish you could feel like a child again, just for a moment? Do you long for that childlike innocence you had so long ago when "visions of sugar plums danced in your head?" Is this belief in the magic and wonder of Christmas a feeling you strive to embrace but always find yourself getting caught up in the added stress and obligations of shopping, decorating, and general overwhelming hustle and bustle of the holiday season?

Well, if this sounds a lot like you, then this year you may want to consider these three ways to bring the true spirit of Christmas back into your heart and mind:

1. REDISCOVER YOUR INNOCENCE

Innocence allows us to be free from the rigid and stale ways of being, all of which inhibit our soul's growth. But because it's so often confused with naiveté, innocence is often not rewarded in our society, a society that puts a high value on criticism and opinion.

True innocence, however, is the opposite of naiveté. We have to be extremely conscious and at peace with ourselves to be free of preconception, judgment, and other harsh behaviors that we so often use to define and secure our identity.

What prevents us from allowing ourselves to become innocent? Is it the fear of looking foolish, of acting like a child rather than an adult? Is it worries that weigh us down so heavily that we feel guilty about setting our minds free to enjoy life for a moment, a day, or the rest of our lives?

When you wish to rediscover your natural way of being, take a deep breath and allow a moment of innocence to fill your heart and mind.

Our souls and spirits always remain in a pure state of innocence.

Be still and take a fresh look at the world through the eyes of a child, the child you once were, and you will believe your innocence is just a breath away.

2. PAY ATTENTION TO MIRACLES

Each time we transform negative thought into positive awareness, we have prepared the ground for a miracle. The world is full of people who, by changing their attitudes, beliefs, and awareness, suddenly begin to experience miracles in their lives. Stories of hope, survival, and inspiring feats of courage are playing out around us all the time. We just have to look.

A superb example of all three—survival, hope, and courage—is the story of a woman who was called "the most positive person in Congress," former United States Representative Gabby Giffords. Congresswoman Giffords survived being shot in the head in 2011. She proved that possibility is without limitation. Even her doctor admitted that "sometimes it's wise just to acknowledge the existence of miracles."

So whether it's as simple as noticing the perfection of a blade of grass, or as astounding as a new beginning in life when all hope appears lost,

all you need is faith "as small as a mustard seed"

that all things are possible no matter how bleak the outlook may seem. Become more aware and appreciative of all the miracles and beauty that surround you, including the miraculous organism that is you. Simply expect a miracle. You won't be disappointed.

3. CREATE YOUR OWN MIRACLES

Giving, caring, and sharing are unbound by social status or monetary wealth. Recall the lyrics to one of our best-loved Christmas carols, "The Little Drummer Boy."

> I have no gift to bring
> I played my drum for Him
> I played my best for Him
> Then He smiled at me.

When we perform acts of kindness, such as donating our time and lending a helping hand to someone who is struggling in some way,

we create a domino effect of positive energy throughout the collective consciousness of the human spirit.

Teach your children and teenagers, who will one day be the leaders of mankind, that we are all, in some way, responsible for each other on this planet.

Think about what you can do to be a shining example to those around you by taking a hot meal or some gently used clothes or toys to families who need a little help. You will create surprises, found treasures, and above all, hope and belief that miracles do happen in all of our lives. Remember that prosperity is not money. Prosperity is a state of being that can be spread to others. It is a feeling.

Holidays are celebrations of love and are meant to inspire each and every one of us to hold pure love and gratitude in our hearts as we touch the lives of others and make the world a better place. So during that very special time of year, and perhaps all the year through, do your best to live your life as an "earthbound angel," and you will feel not only prosperous but magical and wonderful, too!

**LET'S TAKE ACTION!
WORKSHEET:**

How to Rekindle Your Spirit

If you aren't feeling the holiday spirit this season, what are three ways you will bring the true spirit of Christmas back into your heart and mind?

1) _____

_____

_____

2) _____

_____

_____

3) _____

_____

_____

Life Script #58

The Only New Year's *Resolution* You Will Ever Need

The Only New Year's *Resolution* You Will Ever Need

———— • • • ————

Say "goodbye" to fear this year! There's just one New Year's resolution that covers absolutely everything:

HAVE NO FEAR!

If you follow these three steps to detach from fearfulness, you will have smooth sailing in the new year:

1. DON'T GIVE YOUR FEARS ANY POWER

In the movie Defending Your Life, Albert Brooks's character has died and finds himself in the position of defending his own life in court. In this court, he has to account for the times when he allowed his fears to keep him from taking risks that would have brought him success and happiness. The court administers no punishment. If the defendant is found to have too many fears, he or she simply has to go back to earth and try again.

Since fears rarely feature common sense as their primary attribute, the only purpose they serve in our lives is to challenge us to move beyond them. How are you doing so far? Are you an adventurer, an explorer, a discoverer of life? Or would you have a lot to explain in court when asked about the times you wouldn't take that risk and break free from the fears that inhibited your ability to move forward? These are the things that held you back from living your highest potential.

Think of a fear to which you've given power in your life, and ask yourself if it has kept you from doing what your heart may have been leading you to do. Maybe a fear of flying has kept you from the adventure and education of travel. A fear of success may be holding you back from doing your best. Or a fear of letting people know who you truly are might keep you from developing deep friendships or finding a love relationship.

Whatever your focus may be, think of what your life could be like without these fears. Now begin to let them go. You are in charge—not the other way around. Say to yourself, "I am not a prisoner of my fears. They challenge me to live fully. I accept their challenge, and I stand in my power!"

2. LIE ON YOUR BACK AND FLOAT

As we seek personal growth, fear is probably the biggest challenge we encounter. It is the single most effective barrier to our living in a state of peace and joy.

Fortunately, since fear belongs to the realm of the mind, it can be overcome through a change in our thoughts and perceptions.

The primary truth to remember is that fear is almost always projection, not reality. It involves something that might happen or might not happen but that hasn't happened yet. By now, most people are familiar with the acronym:

FEAR is False Evidence Appearing Real.

In a largely futile attempt to know the unknowable, we spend a lot of our time trying to second-guess life. When we start driving ourselves crazy over our inability to control what we have no power to control and no business controlling, it's time to enter into what Zen practitioners term a "don't know mind." In accepting the fact that we can neither know nor control what hasn't happened yet, we free ourselves to concentrate our energies fully on the moment, the only true place of knowing.

Is there something you want to know, or an outcome you want to control and can't? If so, surrender to the moment and get into a state of the "don't know mind." Allow yourself to not know and not care about knowing. Whatever it is will be revealed to you when and if it is supposed to be.

Just remember—you don't know until you know. So just lie back, float, and recall the lyrics to the Beatles song, "Let It Be."

3. DON'T CONNECT TO FEAR

Fear is a place where you don't want to live. Maybe you can't expect to be without fear forever, but you can strive to not connect with it. What's the worst thing that can possibly happen to you if your fears materialize? Play the fear out in your imagination. Be creative. Pull out all the stops. Play it out to the hilt. Then take a deep breath and, on the exhale, release all the fear. Visualize the fear leaving your body and your life. See in your mind's eye a huge pair of scissors, and use them to cut any attachment to the source of this fear.

This year, resolve to forge ahead a path of fearlessness. Realize that by using your inner resources, you will not only have the strength to cope with the worst, but the ingenuity to create the best in your future.

LET'S TAKE ACTION! WORKSHEET:

Time to Cut Your Fears Loose!

Since fears rarely feature common sense as their primary attribute, the only purpose they serve in our lives is to challenge us to move beyond them. How are you doing so far? Are you an adventurer, an explorer, a discoverer of life? Or is your life filled mostly with times you wouldn't take risks or break free from the fears that inhibited your ability to move forward?

Think about a fear you have. Let's play the fear out in your imagination below and on the next pages. What's the worst thing that can possibly happen to you if your fears materialize? Be creative. Pull out all the stops. Play it out to the hilt.

Then take a deep breath and, on the exhale, release all the fear. Visualize the fear leaving your body and your life. See in your mind's eye a huge pair of scissors, and use it to cut any attachment to the source of this fear. Then take an actual scissors and cut your fear loose!

- -

Let Out Your Fears!

Keep Going! →

Now it's time to get your scissors and cut your fears loose! ✂

Congrats!!!

You've completed your course of Life Scripts and taken the first steps along your personal growth journey!

Come back to these prescriptions any time you need a dose of guidance and loving advice.

What To Do Next?!

Leave a Review on Amazon, Please :)

Thank you so much for reading Life Scripts!

If you enjoyed it, I'd really appreciate you leaving a rating and / or review.

It just takes a few seconds.

To get to the review page, just scan the below QR code with your smart phone camera

or go to this link:
https://amzn.to/3BRQclc

Let's Continue Our Journey!

Check out the last page for an
exclusive sneak peek at:

THE
HEALERS TRILOGY

Stay in Touch:

For a free sampling of my next book, giveaways,
collaborations, reviews or latest news, email me!

DonnaLeviBooks@gmail.com

About the Author:

Donna Levi

Author, Donna Levi, has always been interested in spiritual development, metaphysics and philosophy, recognizing life's larger purpose and the necessity for growth and transformation.

While on an educational and spiritual retreat in Arizona, Donna was introduced to the concept of "energy healing" - the belief that a healing energy exists within the human body and mind - which left Donna much to contemplate about our physical existence on this planet. It was the beginning of a journey that would change her life forever.

Months later, Donna became ill and was desperate to get well. As she drifted off to sleep one night, she remembered her experience in Arizona, and knew there must be a way for her to heal herself. In that exact moment, her mind flooded with vivid descriptions of each of the seven amazing characters that eventually would be the foundation for what would become her young adult trilogy. The Healers would be young teachers of mankind, born to spread a message of hope, love, and healing to humanity.

The next morning, Donna felt deeply compelled to begin writing their story. And perhaps not surprisingly, each day that followed, Donna herself moved closer and closer toward perfect health and a full recovery.

Donna has a bachelor's degree in English literature from Vanderbilt University. She lives in Cincinnati, Ohio, and has two wonderful daughters. She is the author of the popular young adult trilogy, The Healers (The Healers, The Healers: Waters of Life, and The Healers: Crystal Caverns). She is also author of the self-help series, Life Scripts: Remedies from One Healer to Another.

You can reach Donna at donnalevibooks@gmail.com

Continue Your Journey
With Donna Levi...

The

HEALERS
TRILOGY:

Also by Donna Levi

The Healers Trilogy:

The Healers
(The Healers Trilogy, Book 1)
Link: https://amzn.to/3amRbib

Waters of Life
(The Healers Trilogy, Book 2)
Link: https://amzn.to/3yTyCvu

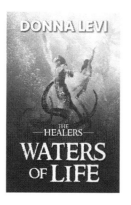

Crystal Caverns
(The Healers Trilogy, Book 3)
Link: https://amzn.to/3yS3fkK

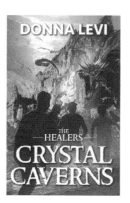